DEFI

Decentralized Finance:
The Future of Finance and Blockchain Technology

Peter J. Owings

Copyright: Copyright by Peter J. Owings

All rights reserved.

This document is geared towards providing exact and reliable information with regards to the topic and issue covered. The publication is sold with the idea that the publisher is not required to render accounting, officially permitted, or otherwise, qualified services. If advice is necessary, legal or professional, a practiced individual in the profession should be ordered.

From a Declaration of Principles which was accepted and approved equally by a Committee of the American Bar Association and a Committee of Publishers and Associations. In no way is it legal to reproduce, duplicate, or transmit any part of this document in either electronic means or in printed format. Recording of this publication is strictly prohibited and any storage of this document is not allowed unless with written permission from the publisher. All rights reserved.

The information provided herein is stated to be truthful and consistent, in that any liability, in terms of inattention or otherwise, by any usage or abuse of any policies, processes, or directions contained within is the solitary and utter responsibility of the recipient reader. Under no circumstances will any legal responsibility or blame be held against the publisher for any reparation, damages, or monetary loss due to the information herein, either directly or indirectly.

Respective authors own all copyrights not held by the publisher.

The information herein is offered for informational purposes solely and is universal as so. The presentation of the information is without contract or any type of guaranteed assurance.

The trademarks that are used are without any consent, and the publication of the trademark is without permission or backing by the trademark owner. All trademarks and brands within this book are for clarifying purposes only and are the owned by the owners themselves, not affiliated with this document.

Disclaimer

All erudition contained in this book is given for informational and educational purposes only. The author is not in any way accountable for any results or outcomes that emanate from using this material. Constructive attempts have been made to

provide information that is both accurate and effective, but the author is not bound for the accuracy or use/misuse of this information.

TABLE OF CONTENTS

Introduction 6
What is DeFi? 6
History of Modern Decentralized Finance 8
DeFi Primitives 24
DeFi Deep Dive 30
Derivatives 36
Problems DeFi Solves 57
Risks associated with DEFI 65
Blockchain technologies on the industry 81
The Structure of Blockchains 90
History of Ethereum 95
The new nature of financial transactions 107
Decentralized applications: Welcome to the future 114
Conclusion 117

INTRODUCTION

WHAT IS DEFI?

"DeFi" is a general term for an evolving trend. Broadly, it is a category of blockchain-based decentralized applications (DApps) for financial services. DeFi encompasses a variety of technologies, business models and organizational structures, generally replacing traditional forms of intermediation. DeFi transactions involve digital assets and generally operate on top of base-layer settlement platforms.

DeFi is primarily a competitive marketplace of decentralised financial applications that serve as various financial "primitives" such as exchange, save, lend, and tokenize. These applications profit from the network effects of combining and recombining DeFi products, gaining market share from the traditional financial ecosystem.

In principle, the first forms of money were not centralised. In exchange for products, agents accepted a variety of objects such as stones or shells. Eventually, specie money arose, a sort of currency with a monetary value. Today, central banks control non-collateralized (fiat) currency. While the shape of money has evolved over time, the fundamental architecture of financial institutions has not.

However, the groundwork is being laid for a historic upheaval to our current financial architecture. Decentralized finance, or DeFi, aims to use blockchain technology to develop and combine open-source financial building blocks into sophisticated products with minimal friction and maximum value to customers. Given that it costs the same to deliver services to a customer with $100 million in assets, we predict DeFi will eventually replace all major centralised financial infrastructure. This is an inclusive technology in which anyone can pay a flat cost to use and profit from DeFi's inventions.

Serious questions remain:

– What, if any, are the distinctive aspects of DeFi? What distinguishes a DeFi service from a similar service based on traditional finance?

– What are the opportunities and potential benefits of DeFi? To whom will these benefits accrue –and who might be excluded or left behind?

– What are the risks – individual, organizational and systemic – of using DeFi? How do these risks apply to clients, markets, counterparties and beyond?

– Can DeFi become a significant alternative to traditional financial services? If so, will there be points of integration? If not, what if anything will DeFi represent in the market?

– What novel legal and policy questions does DeFi raise? How should policy-makers approach DeFi? What options exist for addressing these questions?

This book details the problems that DeFi solves: centralized control, limited access, inefficiency, lack of interoperability, and opacity.

History of Modern Decentralized Finance

While we may argue that today's financial system is riddled with inefficiencies, it is far superior to previous systems. As previously stated, the first market exchanges were peer-to-peer. A barter system needed the exact matching of the demands of two parties. At the same time, and in response to the inefficiency of the barter system, an informal credit system developed in communities, in which people kept a mental record of "gifts."

Coinage appeared much later, approximately in 600 BCE, with the first modern coins in Lydia. These coins served the now-standard purposes of money: unit of account, medium of exchange, and store of value. Durability, mobility, divisibility, uniformity, restricted supply, acceptance, and stability were all important attributes of money. Bank notes, which originated in China, arrived in Europe in the 13th century.

Western Union pioneered non-physical money transfer in 1871.

Credit cards were introduced in 1950 with the Diners Card, ATMs were introduced in 1967 by Barclays Bank, telephone banking was introduced in 1983 by Bank of Scotland, and Internet banking was introduced in 1994 by Stanford Federal Credit Union. Further advancements include RFID payments with Mobil Speedpass (1997), chip and pin credit cards (2005), and Apple Pay (2014).

All of these breakthroughs, it is worth noting, were constructed on the foundation of centralised finance. In fact, the present banking system hasn't altered much in the last 150 years. While digitization was a significant advance, it served to reinforce a heritage system. The significant costs connected with the legacy system prompted additional improvements known as Fintech.

Fintech

When expenses are high, there will be an increase in innovation to profit on inefficiencies. However, a powerful layer of middlemen may stifle innovation. The foreign currency (FX) market was an early example of decentralised finance 20 years ago. Large firms employed investment banks to manage their FX demands at the time. For example, a company situated in the United States may require €50 million by the end of September to complete a payment on items purchased in Germany. Their bank would provide them with a rate for the transaction. Simultaneously, another bank client may need to sell €50 million by the end of September. A separate rate would be quoted by the bank. The difference in rates is known as the spread, and the spread is the profit made by the bank for acting as an intermediary. Given the multi-trillion dollar currency market, this represented a sizable portion of bank profits.

A fintech startup proposed the following idea in early 2001. Rather than having individual firms contact several banks to find the best rate, why not have an electronic system match buyers and sellers directly at an agreed-upon price with no spread? Indeed, the bank may provide this service to its own customers for a small cost (compared to the spread). Furthermore, because some customers have accounts with many banks, it would be able to connect clients at all banks that participate in the peer-to-peer network.

Bitcoin and Cryptocurrency

Beginning in the early 1980s, hundreds of digital money attempts all failed. However, the scene transformed in 2008 with the publishing of the well-known Satoshi Nakamoto Bitcoin white paper. The paper describes a decentralised peer-to-peer system that makes use of the blockchain concept. While Haber and Stornetta invented blockchain in 1991, it was originally intended to be a time-stamping system for keeping track of successive versions of a document. Bitcoin's fundamental innovation was to integrate the concept of blockchain (time stamping) with a consensus mechanism known as Proof of Work (introduced by Back in 2002). The technology created an immutable ledger, which solved a major issue with any digital asset: you could build perfect copies and spend them multiple times.

Blockchains enable the main characteristics desired in a value store, which have never previously been present in a single asset. Blockchains enable cryptographic scarcity (Bitcoin has a fixed supply cap of 21 million coins), censorship resistance, user sovereignty (no entity other than the user may control how funds are used), and mobility (can send any quantity anywhere for a low flat fee). When these characteristics are integrated in a single system, cryptocurrency becomes a strong invention.

The value proposal of Bitcoin is critical to comprehend, and it can be placed into context by examining the value propositions of other financial instruments. Take, for example, the US dollar. Prior to the removal of the gold standard in 1971, it was backed by gold. The demand for USD now stems from three sources: 1) taxes; 2) purchases of US goods denominated in USD; and 3) debt repayment denominated in USD. None of these three situations generate intrinsic value; rather, they generate value depending on the network that is the US economy. The expansion or contraction of various components of the US economy can have an impact on the USD's price. Furthermore, changes in the supply of USD affect its price at a given level of demand. The Fed can use monetary policy to modify the supply of USD in order to achieve financial or political objectives. Inflation erodes the value of the US dollar, reducing its ability to store value over time. One might be concerned about rapid inflation, dubbed "The Great Monetary Inflation" by Paul Tudor Jones, which would cause a flight to inflation-resistant assets.

Because of its virtually restricted supply, actual utility, and overall global dependability, gold has proven to be a successful inflation hedge. However, because gold is a volatile asset, its historical hedging ability is realised only over relatively long time horizons.

Many believe that because bitcoin has no "tangible" value, it should be worthless. Continuing with the gold example, roughly two-thirds of gold is used for jewelry, with the remainder being used in technology hardware. Gold has a monetary worth. While a fiat currency, the US dollar has value as "legal tender." However, there are several cases throughout history of currency emerging with no backing that had value.

The Iraqi Swiss dinar is a more recent example. This was Iraq's currency until the first Gulf War in 1990. The printing plates were made in Switzerland (thus the name), and the printing was done in the United Kingdom. Iraq was divided in 1991, with the Kurds holding the north and Saddam Hussien dominating the south. Due to restrictions, Iraq was unable to import dinars and was forced to begin domestic manufacturing. The Central Bank of Iraq announced in May 1993 that citizens had three weeks to exchange their old 25 dinars for new ones.

Ethereum and DeFi

Ethereum (ETH) is now the second most valuable cryptocurrency in terms of market capitalization ($230 billion). Vitalik Buterin proposed the idea in 2014, and the first block of Ethereum was mined in 2015. In some ways, Ethereum is a logical extension of Bitcoin's applications. It enables smart contracts, which are pieces of code that live on a blockchain and can control assets and data as well as define interactions between assets, data, and network participants. Ethereum is defined as a smart contract platform by its ability to support smart contracts.

The decentralised application, or dApp, was created expressly by Ethereum and other smart contract platforms. The backend components of these applications are built with interoperable, transparent smart contracts that exist as long as the chain on which they live does. dApps enable peers to interact directly, eliminating the need for a company to act as a clearing house for app interactions. It became clear early on that the first killer dApps would be pecuniary in nature.

The push for financial dApps spawned a new movement known as decentralised finance, or DeFi. DeFi's goal is to create and combine open-source financial building blocks into sophisticated products with minimal friction and maximum value to users. DeFi proponents believe that all meaningful financial infrastructure will be replaced by smart contracts that can provide more value to a larger group of users because it costs no more at an organizational level to provide services to a customer with $100 or $100 million in assets. Anyone can use the contract and profit from DeFi's innovations by simply paying the flat price.

DeFi is primarily a competitive marketplace of financial dApps that perform various financial "primitives" such as exchange, lend, tokenize, and so on. These dApps benefit from the network effects of combining and recombining DeFi goods, gaining market share from the traditional financial ecosystem. Our goal is to provide an overview of the challenges DeFi solves, a description of the current rapidly expanding DeFi ecosystem, and a vision of the future prospects that DeFi opens up.

DeFi Infrastructure

The decentralising backbone, a blockchain, is the cornerstone to all DeFi. Blockchains are simply software protocols that enable multiple parties to function under shared assumptions and data without having to trust each other. These data can be anything, e.g., the position and destination of things in a supply chain or the balance of a token's account. Updates are bundled into "blocks" and cryptographically "chained" together to allow an audit of earlier history, hence the name.

A Consensus Protocol, a set of rules that define what types of blocks can become part of the chain and constitute the "truth," is what makes blockchains feasible. Up to a given security constraint, these consensus techniques are supposed to be resistant to malicious tampering. The blockchains we are interested in use the Proof of Work (PoW) consensus system, which uses a computationally demanding lottery to decide which block to add. The participants agree that the truth is the longest chain of blocks. If an attacker wishes to create a longer chain of malicious transactions, they must outperform the entire network's computational work. In theory, they would require a majority of the network power to accomplish this, which is why the famous 51 percent attack is the limit of PoW security. Fortunately, amassing this much network power on the most widely used blockchains, such as Bitcoin or Ethereum, is extremely difficult for any individual, let alone an entire country. Even if a majority of network power ("hashrate") can be obtained briefly, the amount of block history that can be overwritten is limited by how long this majority can be maintained.

While we are focusing on Proof of Work, there are several other consensus methods, the most important of which being Proof of Stake (PoS). Validators in Proof of Stake commit some capital (the stake) to verify that the block is valid. Validators make their cryptocurrency available by staking it, and they may be chosen to propose a block. A majority of the other validators must attest to the proposed block. Validators benefit from both offering a block and attesting to the validity of other people's suggested blocks.

As long as no malicious party gains majority control of the network's processing capacity, transactions will be processed and appended to the ledger when a block is "won."

Cryptocurrency

Cryptocurrency is the most widely used application of blockchain technology. Cryptocurrency is a token (typically rare) that is encrypted and transferred. Scarcity is what ensures the possibility of value, and it is also a blockchain invention. Digital things, in general, are easily replicated. "[Bitcoin] is a wonderful cryptographic achievement, and the potential to build something that is not duplicable in the digital world has enormous value," stated Eric Schmidt, former CEO of Google.

Due to the asymmetric key cryptography that protects the accounts, no one may publish a fraudulent transaction unless they possess the matching account. You have one "public" key that represents an address for receiving tokens and another "private" key that is used to unlock and spend tokens that you have custody over. When you use the internet, the same type of cryptography is used to protect your credit card information and data. A single account cannot "double-spend" their tokens because the ledger keeps an audit of their balance at all times, and the erroneous transaction would not be cleared.

The ability to avoid "double-spending" without the intervention of a central authority exemplifies the major benefit of employing a blockchain to maintain the underlying ledger.

The Bitcoin blockchain was the first cryptocurrency model, and it acts almost entirely as a payment network, capable of storing and transferring bitcoins across the globe in real-time with no intermediaries or censorship. This is the potent value proposition that gives bitcoin its monetary value. Despite its tremendous network effects, technology competitors provide better functionality.

The Smart Contract Platform

A smart contract platform is an essential component of DeFi. These blockchains go beyond a simple payment network like Bitcoin and allow for the generation of smart contracts that improve the chain's capabilities. Ethereum is the most well-known example of a smart contract platform. A smart contract is a piece of code that can generate and transform arbitrary data or tokens on top of the blockchain. The notion is powerful because it enables the user to confidently encode rules for any form of transaction and even to create scarce assets with specific functionality. Many traditional business agreement clauses could be shifted to a smart contract, which would not only enumerate but also algorithmically enforce those clauses. Smart contracts have applications beyond finance, including gaming, data stewardship, and supply chain management, among others.

The existence of a transaction fee known as a gas fee is an interesting caveat that applies to Ethereum but not necessarily to all smart contract platforms. Consider Ethereum to be a massive computer with numerous applications (smart contracts). If a person wants to use the computer, they must pay a price for each unit of computing used. A simple computation, such as sending ETH, necessitates only minor effort in updating a few account balances. There is a minor petrol price for this. A sophisticated computation that includes minting tokens and testing numerous conditions across multiple contracts costs more gas. An automobile is a good analogy for Ethereum. To drive a car, a certain amount of gas is required, and there is a fee to obtain the gas. However, the gas fee may result in a poor user experience. The gas price requires agents to keep an ETH balance in order to pay it, and they must be concerned not only about overspending, but also about underpaying and having the transaction fail entirely.

As a result, efforts are ongoing to abstract gas payments from end users and enable competing networks that fully eliminate the concept of gas. However, gas is vital as a fundamental technique for mitigating system attacks that generate an unending loop of code. It is not possible to detect malicious code of this type before to running it, a problem known formally in computer science as the stopping problem. By making such attacks prohibitively expensive, gas secures the Ethereum network.

Continuing with our analogy, gas solves the stopping problem as follows: Assume a "vehicle" is on autopilot and is running at full power with no driver. Because the car has to stop eventually when the petrol tank runs out, gas functions as a limiting factor. This encourages extremely efficient smart contract development since contracts that consume fewer resources and lower the likelihood of user failures have a far higher chance of being used and prospering in the market. On a smart contract platform, the options quickly outnumber what developers looking to integrate multiple applications can easily handle. As a result, standard interfaces for various sorts of functionality are being used. These standards are known as Ethereum Request for Comments on Ethereum (ERC). The most well-known of them specify various types of tokens with comparable functionality. ERC-20 is the standard for fungible tokens; it defines an interface for tokens whose utility and functionality units are equal. It comprises actions such as transferring units and authorising operators to use a portion of a user's balance. ERC-721, the non-fungible token standard, is another well-known token. ERC-721 tokens are one-of-a-kind and are frequently used for collectibles or assets such as peer-to-peer lending. The advantage of these standards is that application developers can write a code for a single interface and support every token that implements that interface.

Oracles

The fact that blockchain technologies are insulated from the world outside of their ledger is an intriguing problem. That is, the Ethereum blockchain only knows what is going on the Ethereum blockchain and not, for example, the level of the S&P 500 or which team won the Super Bowl. This limitation, known as the oracle problem, restricts applications to Ethereum native contracts and tokens, diminishing the usability of the smart contract platform. In the context of smart contract platforms, an oracle is any data source that reports information from outside the block chain. How can we build an oracle that can speak authoritatively about off chain data while minimizing trust? Many applications necessitate the use of an oracle, and implementations differ in their degree of centralization.

Oracles are used in various DeFi applications in a variety of ways. A popular solution is for an application to host its own oracle or to connect to an existing oracle hosted by a reliable platform. Chainlink, an Ethereum-based network, is aimed to overcome the oracle problem by aggregating data sources. The Chainlink whitepaper contains a reputation-based system that has yet to be implemented. We go through the oracle problem in further detail later. Oracles are undoubtedly an open design topic and a difficulty for DeFi to gain value outside of its own isolated chain.

Stable coins

Excessive volatility is a critical flaw with many cryptocurrencies. This complicates things for consumers that want to use DeFi applications but don't have the risk tolerance for a volatile asset like ETH. To address this, a new cryptocurrency class known as Stablecoins has arisen.

Stablecoins are designed to maintain price parity with a specific asset, such as the US dollar or gold. Stablecoins provide the needed stability for investors to participate in various DeFi applications, as well as a cryptocurrency native solution for exiting positions in more volatile crypto assets. They can also be used to provide on-chain exposure to off-chain asset returns if the target asset is not native to the underlying blockchain (e.g., gold, stocks, ETFs). The process through which the Stablecoin maintains its peg differs depending on the implementation.

Fiat-collateralized, crypto-collateralized, and non-collateralized Stablecoins are the three basic mechanisms.

Fiat-collateralized Stablecoins are by far the most common type of Stablecoin. These are collateralized by an off-chain reserve of the target asset. Typically, these are held by an external business or set of entities, which are subjected to routine audits to ensure the collateral's existence. Tether (USDT) is the largest fiat-collateralized Stablecoin, with a market capitalization of $24 billion dollars, making it the third largest cryptocurrency behind Bitcoin and Ethereum at the time of writing. Tether has the most trading volume of any cryptocurrency, yet it is not audited. The second-largest is USDC, which is backed by Coinbase and is audited. On Coinbase's exchange, USDC can be redeemed 1:1 for USD and vice versa for no cost. As there is a significant need for Stablecoin investment opportunities, USDT and USDC are particularly popular to include into DeFi protocols. However, there is an inherent risk with these tokens because they are centrally controlled and have the ability to block accounts.

Crypto-collateralized Stablecoins are the second most common type of Stablecoin. These are Stablecoins that are backed by an amount of another cryptocurrency that has been overcollateralized. Depending on the arrangement, their value can be hard or soft tied to the underlying asset. The most widely used crypto-collateralized Stablecoin is DAI, which was developed by MakerDAO and is backed mostly by ETH with collateral support for a few other crypto assets. It is soft pegged by economic mechanisms that encourage supply and demand to drive the price to $1. As of this writing, DAI has a market capitalization of $1 billion. We'll get deep into MakerDAO and DAI. sUSD is another popular crypto collateralized Stablecoin. This is a platform feature of Synthetix. It is backed by the Synthetix network token (SNX) and is fixed to one US dollar via its exchange functionality.

The benefits of crypto-collateralized Stablecoins include decentralisation and secured collateral. The disadvantage is that their scalability is restricted. To manufacture more Stablecoins, a user must back the issuance with an overcollateralized debt position. In other circumstances, such as DAI, there is also a debt ceiling, which further restricts supply expansion.

Non-collateralized Stablecoins are the final and probably most intriguing class of Stablecoins. These are not backed by any underlying asset and rely on algorithmic supply expansion and contraction to change the price to the peg. They frequently use a seigniorage model, in which token holders on the platform receive an increase in supply when demand rises. When demand falls and the price falls below the peg, these platforms will issue bonds of some kind, entitling the holder to future expansionary supply before token holders receive their portion. This mechanism is essentially identical to the one of central banks associated with fiat currencies, with the exception that these platforms have the stated objective of tying the price rather than supporting government spending or other economic goals. Basis is a notable early example of an algorithmic stable coin that was forced to close owing to regulatory issues. Ampleforth (AMPL) and Empty Set Dollar are two current instances of algorithmic stable coins (ESD). The disadvantage of non-collateralized stable coins is that they lack inherent underlying value to support the exchange of their token. This can result in "bank runs" in contractions, where the majority of holders are left with enormous sums of the token that are no longer worth the peg price.

The creation of a decentralised stable coin that both scales effectively and is resistant to collapse in contractions is still a work in progress. There are also regulatory concerns, which we shall address later. Stable coins are a crucial component of the DeFi infrastructure since they let users to benefit from the applications' functionality without incurring excessive price volatility.

Decentralized Applications

As previously stated, dApps are an important DeFi component. dApps are comparable to regular software apps, with the exception that they run on a decentralised smart contract framework. The key advantage of these programs is their lack of permission and resistance to censorship. They can be used by anyone, and no single entity has control over them. A decentralised autonomous organization is a distinct but related idea (DAO). The rules of functioning of a DAO are contained in smart contracts, which specify who can execute what behavior or upgrade. A governance token, which grants an owner a percentage of the vote on future outcomes, is prevalent in a DAO.

DEFI will change the problems of Centralized Financial Systems

We have lived in a world of centralized finance for generations. The supply of money is controlled by central banks. Financial trade is mostly done through middlemen. Traditional banking organizations handle borrowing and lending. However, in recent years, significant work has been made on a very different paradigm - decentralised finance, or DeFi. Peers engage with one another in this system via a shared ledger that is not controlled by any centralised body.

DeFi has significant promise for addressing the five major issues connected with centralised finance:

1. **Centralized control.**

There are numerous stages to centralization. The majority of individuals and businesses work with a single, localized bank. Rates and fees are set by the bank. It is feasible to switch, but it can be pricey. Furthermore, the banking system in the United States is heavily consolidated. The four largest banks now account for 44 percent of insured deposits, up from 15 percent in the late 1990s. Surprisingly, the banking sector in the United States is less consolidated than in other countries such as the United

Kingdom and Canada. A single centralised institution attempts to determine short-term interest rates and influence the rate of inflation in a centralised banking system. The phenomenon of centralization is not limited to the legacy financial sector.

2. Limited access

Today, 1.7 billion individuals are unbanked, making it difficult for them to receive loans and do business on the internet. Furthermore, many customers are forced to rely on pay-day loan businesses to make ends meet. Being banked, on the other hand, does not ensure access. A bank, for example, may not want to bother with the little loan that a fledgling firm requires, and instead may recommend a credit card loan. The credit card might have an annual borrowing rate much above 25%, posing a substantial barrier to identifying viable investment ventures.

3. Inefficiency

There are numerous inefficiencies in a centralised financial system. The credit card interchange rate is perhaps the most severe example, as it leads consumers and small companies to lose up to 3% of a transaction's value with every swipe due to the payment network oligopoly's pricing dominance. Fees for remittances range from 5-7 percent. Another example is the two days it takes to "settle" a stock transaction (officially transfer ownership). This seems completely absurd in the age of the internet.

Other inefficiencies include costly (and time-consuming) capital transfers, direct and indirect brokerage fees, a lack of security, and the inability to execute microtransactions. Many of these inefficiencies are hidden from users. Deposit interest rates remain very low in the existing banking system, but loan interest rates remain quite high, as banks must cover their brick-and-mortar expenditures. In the insurance industry we face similar problems.

4. **Lack of interoperability**

Consumers and businesses interact with financial institutions in an environment where interconnectivity is restricted. Our banking system is compartmentalized and structured to keep switching costs high. Transferring funds from one institution to another can be time-consuming and complicated. It can take up to three days to execute a wire transfer. This is a well-known issue, and some efforts are being made to address it. Visa's proposed acquisition of Plaid in 2019 is a recent example. Plaid enables any enterprise, with the user's agreement, to connect to a financial institution's information stack. This is an example of a firm in the area of centralised finance attempting to purchase a product to ameliorate a specific problem while failing to address the basic issues with the current financial infrastructure. It was a calculated move to purchase time.

5. **Information Asymmetry**

The current financial system is opaque. Customers have little information about their bank's financial condition and must rely on the limited government protection of FDIC insurance on their accounts. Bank consumers looking for a loan have a tough time determining whether the given rate is competitive. Although the consumer insurance industry has made some progress with fintech firms that offer to find the "lowest" pricing, the lending market is very fragmented. The present list of competing lenders, on the other hand, is plagued by system inefficiencies. As a result, the "lowest" price still includes legacy brick-and-mortar expenditures as well as bloated back-office fees.

The consequences of these five issues are dual. For starters, many of these costs reduce economic growth. For example, as previously discussed, if loan rates are high due to legacy expenses, high-quality investment projects may be avoided. A high-quality proposal from an entrepreneur may aim for a 20% rate of return, exactly the type of project that promotes economic growth. If the bank advises the entrepreneur to borrow money on her credit card at a rate of 24 percent per year, this lucrative project may never be pursued.

Second, these issues maintain and/or increase inequality. Most people (from all political stripes) believe that there should be equality of opportunity: a project should be funded based on the quality of the idea and the soundness of the execution plan, not on other variables. Importantly, when brilliant ideas are not funded, inequality inhibits growth. While claiming to be the "country of opportunity," the United States has one of the worst records in terms of moving income from the bottom to the top quartiles. Inequality of opportunity stems, in part, from a lack of access to the present banking system, reliance on expensive alternative financing such as payday lending, and an inability to buy or sell in the modern world of e-commerce. These consequences are far-reaching, and by any calculation, this is a long list of major problems that are inherent in our existing centralised financial system. Despite the fact that we are living in the digital age, our financial infrastructure has yet to fully embrace it. Decentralized finance opens up new possibilities. The technology is still in its early stages, but the potential is exciting.

DeFi Primitives

Now that we've built the framework by defining the DeFi infrastructure, we'll cover the basic financial activities that developers can use in this chapter. These actions can be used by a developer to create complicated dApps. We will go through each of the primitive actions in depth, as well as the advantages they may offer over their centralised equivalents.

Transactions

Ethereum transactions are the building blocks of DeFi (and Ethereum as a whole). Transactions entail the transfer of data and/or ETH (or other tokens) from one address to another. Every Ethereum interaction, including the primitives covered in this section, starts with a transaction.

As a result, understanding the mechanics of transactions is critical to understanding Ethereum in particular and DeFi in general. An Ethereum user can manage addresses by using an externally owned account (EOA) or smart contract code (contract account). When information is provided to a contract account, it is used to execute code in that contract. The transaction may or may not include an ETH payment for the contract's use. Transactions to an EOA can only send ETH. A single transaction begins with an end-user from an EOA, but it may interact with a huge number of dApps (or any Ethereum smart contract) before it is completed. The transaction begins by engaging with a single contract, which enumerates all of the intermediate steps in the transaction that must be performed within the contract body.

Transactions carry a gas fee, which fluctuates depending on the transaction's complexity. When ETH is used to reward a miner for including and processing a transaction, for example, the gas charge is relatively modest. Transactions that are longer or more data-intensive cost more gas. If a transaction fails for any reason or runs out of gas, the miner loses all gas used up to that point. Forfeiture protects miners who, in the absence of this measure, could be subjected to massive volumes of failed transactions for which they would not be compensated. The market determines the gas price, which effectively establishes an auction for inclusion in the next Ethereum block. Increased gas prices indicate higher demand and, as a result, higher priority for inclusion.

A technical note concerning transactions: they are submitted to a memory pool, or mempool, before being added to a block. Miners watch for these posted transactions, add them to their own mempool, and share them with other miners so that they can be included in the next available block.

If the transaction's gas price is uncompetitive in comparison to other transactions in the mempool, the transaction is delayed to a later block. By running or connecting with mining nodes, any actor can see transactions in the mempool. This visibility can even enable improved front-running and other competitive strategies that help the miner profit from trading activities. If a miner notices a transaction in the mempool that she may profit from by either executing it herself or front-running it, she is incentivized to do so if she is lucky enough to win the block. Any instance of direct execution is referred to as miner extractable value (MEV). MEV is a disadvantage of the proof-of-work model. Certain tactics, such as obfuscating transactions, can mitigate MEV by concealing how miners may profit from the transactions.

Fungible Tokens

Fungible tokens are a key component of Ethereum and DeFi's value proposition. Any Ethereum developer can build a token that is divisible to a specific decimal granularity and has identical and interchangeable units. USD, for example, is a fungible asset since one $100 dollar equals one hundred $1 bills. ERC-20 is the Ethereum blockchain token interface. From the standpoint of an application developer, an interface is the bare minimum of functionality. When a token implements the ERC-20 interface, any application that handles the stated functions generically can integrate with the token instantaneously and effortlessly. Application developers can securely support tokens that do not yet exist by using ERC-20 and related APIs.

Transfers with insufficient balances or unlawful spending will be rejected by the contract. The first four functions are self-explanatory and expected (reading supply, balances, and sending tokens). The last two functions, approve and allowance, are crucial to comprehending the ERC-20 interface's power. Users would be confined to directly transferring tokens to and from accounts if this function did not exist.

Contracts (or trusted accounts) can be whitelisted with approval capability to act as custodians for a user's tokens without actually holding the token balance. Because users retain full custody before an approved spender executes a transaction, this functionality broadens the range of viable applications.

Equity Token

An equity token is just a token that reflects ownership of an underlying asset or pool of assets. It is not to be confused with equities or stocks in the traditional finance sense. The units must be fungible in order for each to correspond to the same portion of the pool. Assume a token, TKN, has a total fixed quantity of 10,000, and TKN equates to a 100-ETH pool stored in a smart contract. The smart contract specifies that for each unit of TKN received, it will return a pro rata amount of ETH, with the exchange ratio set at 100 TKN/1 ETH.

We may modify the example so that the pool contains a variable quantity of ETH. Assume the ETH in the pool grows at a rate of 5% per year by some other process. Now, 100 TKN would be equivalent to 1 ETH plus a 5% perpetual cash flow of ETH. This information can be used by the market to accurately price the worth of TKN.

The pools of assets in true equity tokens can incorporate far more complicated dynamics, going beyond a static pool or defined rates of increase. Only what can be encoded into a smart contract limits the possibilities.

Utility Tokens

Utility tokens are, in many ways, a catch-all category, despite having a clear definition. Utility tokens are fungible tokens that are required to use a smart contract system's functionality or that have an intrinsic value proposition defined by its respective smart contract system.

Utility tokens drive the economics of a system in many circumstances, producing scarcity or incentives where the developers intended. In some circumstances, ETH might be used instead of a utility token, however utility tokens allow systems to accumulate and retain economic value that is not tied to Ethereum as a whole. A system with algorithmically varying supply is an example of a use case that necessitates the employment of a separate utility token.

Governance Tokens

Governance tokens are analogous to equity tokens in that they reflect a proportion of ownership. Governance token ownership, as the name implies, applies to voting rights rather than assets. We begin by inspiring owners to vote on the types of changes they want.

Many smart contracts include provisions that specify how the system might change; for example, authorised changes could include tweaking parameters, adding new components, or changing the functionality of current components. Given the likelihood that the contract with which a user interacts today may change tomorrow, the system's flexibility to evolve is a powerful offer. In other circumstances, only developer admins who have encoded unique privileges for themselves can control platform updates.

Because of the centralised control of the admins, any platform with admin-controlled functionality is not truly DeFi. A contract without the ability to alter, on the other hand, is necessarily rigid and has no way of adapting to defects in the code or changing economic or technical conditions. As a result, many systems aspire towards a decentralised upgrade process, which is frequently mediated by a governance token.

Owners of a governance token would have pro-rata voting rights to enact any change permitted by the platform's smart contracts.

A governance token can be implemented in a variety of ways, including with a static supply, an inflationary supply, or even a deflationary supply. A static supply is simple: acquired shares correspond directly to a particular percentage of the vote. The present MakerDAO implementation of the MKR coin has a mostly unchanging supply.

Nonfungible Tokens

The ERC-721 standard on Ethereum defines nonfungibility. This standard is identical to ERC-20, except that instead of all units being recorded as a single balance, each unit has its own unique ID. This distinct ID can be linked to extra metadata that distinguishes the token from others derived from the same contract. The balance Of(address) method returns the total quantity of nonfungible tokens (NFTs) owned by the address in the provided contract. An extra function, ownerOf(id), returns the address's ownership of a specific token specified by its ID. Another significant distinction is that ERC-20 allows for partial approval of an operator's token holdings, but ERC-721 is all-or-nothing. Any of the NFTs can be moved by an operator who has been authorised to use them.

In DeFi, NFTs offer fascinating uses. Their other name, deeds, implies that they are used to symbolise unique ownership of unitary assets, for example, ownership of a specific P2P loan with its own rates and terms. After that, the asset may be transferred and sold using the ERC721 interface. Another application could be to represent a lottery ticket. Lottery tickets may be called nonfungible since only one or a small number of them will be winning tickets, leaving the remainder worthless. NFTs also have a compelling use case in their capacity to bridge financial and nonfinancial use cases through collectibles (e.g., a token could represent ownership in a piece of art). NFTs can also represent scarce items in a game or other network and retain economic worth in NFT secondary marketplaces.

DeFi Deep Dive

DeFi can be divided into sectors based on the functionality of the dApp. Because many dApps may fit into numerous categories, we try to place them in the most relevant one. We investigate DeFi platforms via the lens of lending/credit facilities, DEXes, derivatives, and tokenization.

Credit/Lending

MakerDAO (decentralised autonomous organization) is frequently cited as an example of DeFi. MakerDAO's major value-add is the establishment of a crypto-collateralized Stablecoin linked to USD. This means that the system may operate entirely within the Ethereum blockchain, with no reliance for external centralised institutions to support, vault, or audit the Stablecoin. MakerDAO is a two-token paradigm in which a governance token MKR grants platform voting rights and participates in value capture. The second token is DAI, a Stablecoin that is a cornerstone in the DeFi ecosystem and is used by numerous protocols, including a few we shall examine later.

DAI is generated in the following manner. A user can deposit ETH or other ERC-20-compliant assets into a Vault. A Vault is a smart contract that escrows collateral and keeps track of the collateral's USD-denominated value. The user can then mint DAI on their assets up to a specific collateralization ratio. This results in a "debt" in DAI that must be repaid by the Vault holder. The comparable asset is the DAI, which can be used anyway the Vault holder sees fit. For example, the user might sell the DAI for cash or leverage it into more of the collateral asset18, and then repeat the process. Due to the volatility of ETH and most collateral forms, the collateralization need exceeds 100 percent and is typically in the 150-200 percent range.

The fundamental concept is not novel; it is essentially a collateralized loan position. For example, a homeowner in need of cash can pledge their home as security to a bank and acquire a mortgage loan with a cash takeout. Because the price volatility of ETH is substantially larger than that of a house, the collateralization ratios for the ETH-DAI contract are higher. Furthermore, no centralised organization is required because everything takes place on the Ethereum blockchain.

The viability of the MakerDAO ecosystem is fundamentally dependent on DAI remaining pegged to the USD at a 1:1 ratio. Various methods have been put in place to stimulate demand and supply in order to move the price closer to the peg. The debt cap, stability fee, and DAI Savings Rate are the principal mechanisms for sustaining the peg (DSR). Holders of the governance token Maker (MKR) and MakerDAO governance, which we shall describe near the end of this section, control these parameters.

The Stability Fee is a variable interest rate that Vault holders pay in DAI on any DAI debt they generate. To promote the generation or repayment of DAI and move its price toward the peg, the interest rate can be raised or dropped (even to a negative value). The DSR, a variable rate that any DAI holder can earn on their DAI deposit, is funded by the Stability Fee. The DSR is calculated on a per-block basis. The smart contracts that power the platform enforce the Stability Fee, which must always be larger than or equal to the DSR. Finally, a DAI debt ceiling enforced by a smart contract can be changed to allow for more or less supply to satisfy current demand. When the protocol reaches the debt ceiling, no more DAI can be coined in new Vaults until the previous debt is paid off or the ceiling is increased.

To keep the DAI safely collateralized, a user can deposit more collateral into the Vault to stay above the liquidation level. When a position is assessed to be below the liquidation ratio, the keeper can launch an auction (sell some of the ETH collateral19) to liquidate the position and close the Vault holder's obligation. The Liquidation Penalty is computed as a percentage of the debt and is deducted from the collateral together with the money required to close the transaction.

Any remaining collateral reverts to the Vault owner following the sale. The Liquidation Penalty incentivizes market participants to monitor the Vaults and initiate an auction when a position becomes undercollateralized. If the collateral's value falls so low that the DAI debt cannot be fully returned, the position is closed, and the protocol incurs Protocol Debt. There is a DAI buffer pool to cover Protocol Debt, but in some cases the debt can be too large for even the buffer pool to cover. The governance token MKR and the governance system are involved in the solution.

MakerDAO is controlled by the MKR token. Token holders have the ability to vote on protocol improvements, such as supporting additional collateral kinds and adjusting parameters like collateralization ratios. MKR holders are expected to make decisions that benefit the platform financially. Their interest is that a healthy platform will improve the value of their governance stake in the platform. Poor governance, for example, could result in the situation outlined above, in which the buffer pool is insufficient to repay the Protocol Debt. In this situation, newly generated MKR tokens are auctioned off for DAI, and the DAI are used to repay the Protocol Debt. This is the Global Settlement process, a fail-safe method designed to be used only when all other measures have failed. The MKR share is diluted by Global Settlement, which is why stakeholders are driven to avoid it and maintain Protocol Debt to a minimum.

MakerDAO's future is collectively owned by MKR holders. A proposal and the corresponding authorised vote can alter any of the platform's parameters. Other probable parameter modifications include Vaults supporting new collateral kinds and adding functionality upgrades. MKR investors, for example, might decide to pay themselves a dividend funded by the difference between Vault interest payments and the DAI Savings Rate. The benefit of getting this dividend would have to be balanced against any unfavorable community reaction (for example, a backlash against rent seeking from a previously no-rent system) that could reduce the value of the protocol and the MKR token. DAI is appealing to users due of a number of advantages. Users can also buy and use DAI without having to go through the process of producing it in a Vault—they can simply buy DAI on an exchange. As a result, consumers are not required to understand the fundamental mechanics of how DAI are formed. By using the protocol, holders can simply earn the DAI Savings Rate. More technologically and financially capable users can use the MakerDAO web site to establish Vaults and create DAI in order to obtain liquidity from their assets without selling them. To obtain leverage, it is simple to sell DAI and purchase an additional amount of the collateral asset.

Compound is a lending market that provides a variety of ERC-20 assets for borrowing and lending. All tokens in a single market are pooled together, such that every lender earns and every borrower pays the same variable rate.

The concept of a credit rating is useless, and because Ethereum accounts are pseudonymous, it is nearly impossible to enforce repayment in the case of a loan default. As a result, all loans are overcollateralized in a collateral asset other than the one borrowed. If a borrower's collateralization ratio falls below a certain threshold, their position is liquidated to pay off their loan. A keeper, similar to the mechanism employed in MakerDAO Vaults, can liquidate the debt. For each unit of debt closed out, the keeper receives a bonus incentive.

A collateral factor is used to compute the collateralization ratio. Each ERC-20 asset on the platform has its own collateral factor, which ranges from 0% to 90%. When the collateral factor is zero, an asset cannot be used as collateral. For a single collateral type, the needed collateralization ratio is computed as 100 divided by the collateral factor. Volatile assets typically have lower collateral factors, necessitating larger collateralization ratios due to the increased risk of a price movement leading to undercollateralization. When numerous collateral kinds are used by an account at the same time, the collateralization ratio is computed as 100 divided by the weighted average of the collateral types by their relative sizes (denominated in a common currency) in the portfolio.

The collateralization ratio, which is analogous to a reserve multiplier in traditional banking, limits the amount of "borrowed" dollars that can be in the system in relation to the "actual" supply. For example, there is sometimes more DAI in Compound than is supplied by MakerDAO, because users borrow and refill or sell to others who resupply. Importantly, all MakerDAO production is eventually secured by genuine collateral, with no way to borrow more collateral value than has been issued.

Aave

Aave (introduced in 2017) is a lending market protocol that is similar to Compound but has several more capabilities. Aave provides far more tokens for supply and borrowing than Compound does. At the time of writing, Compound offers eight separate tokens (various ERC20 Ethereum-based assets), but Aave offers these eight plus an extra nine that Compound does not offer. Importantly, unlike the volatile COMP token in Compound, there is no subsidy involved with Aave lending and variable borrowing rates.

The Aave protocol encourages the creation of wholly new marketplaces. Each market has its own set of token pools, each with its own set of supply and borrow interest rates. The advantage of creating a distinct market is that the market's supported tokens operate as collateral only in that market and cannot affect other markets, thereby minimising any contagion. Aave now operates in two major markets. The first is for more traditional ERC-20 tokens, such as those used by Compound, which support assets such as ETH, USDC, and DAI. The second applies just to Uniswap LP tokens. When a user puts collateral into a Uniswap market, for example, she receives an LP token which reflects her ownership in the market. To earn further returns, the LP tokens can be put in Aave's Uniswap market.

To execute a flash loan, Aave levies a fee of 9 basis points (bps) on the loan amount. Because each provider owns a pro rata portion of the pool, the fee is paid to the asset pool and provides an additional return on investment. One key application for flash loans is that they provide users with quick access to funds in order to refinance holdings. This functionality is critical to DeFi, both as a general infrastructure component and as part of a great user experience (UX).

Aave is working on a Credit Delegation feature that would allow users to provide collateral to potential borrowers who can then use it to borrow a desired asset. The method is unsafe and is based on trust. This technique allows for uncollateralized loan connections, similar to those seen in traditional finance, and has the ability to open the floodgates in terms of liquidity sources. To compensate for the risk of unsecured loans, credit delegation agreements will almost certainly include fees and credit scores.

Finally, the delegator has sole discretion in determining who is a qualified borrower and what contract terms are adequate. Credit delegation terms, for example, can be handled by a smart contract.

Alternatively, the delegated liquidity can be given to a smart contract, which can then use the liquidity to perform the required function. The fundamental advantage of credit delegation is that all loans in Aave are ultimately secured by collateral, regardless of who owns the asset.

To summarise, Aave goes above and beyond the loan options given by Compound and other competitors. Although not unique among competitors, Aave's flash loans provide additional income to investors, making it a tempting technique for providing liquidity. These utilities are also appealing to platform arbitrageurs and other applications that require instant liquidity for their use cases. Stable borrow rates are a critical innovation, and Aave is the only platform that now provides this service. This feature may be useful for larger players who cannot operate under the possible instability of fluctuating interest rates.

DERIVATIVES

Yield Protocol

Yield Protocol presents a derivative model for zero-coupon secured bonds. The protocol specifies a yToken as an ERC-20 (fungible) token that settles in a defined quantity of a target asset at a given date. The contract will state that tokens with the same expiry date, target asset, collateral asset, and collateralization ratio are fungible. The tokens are collateralized by the collateral asset and have a needed maintenance collateralization ratio, similar to MakerDAO and other DeFi platforms we've explored. If the collateral's value falls below the required level of maintenance, the position can be liquidated by selling some or all of the collateral to cover the debt.

dYdX

dYdX is a firm that focuses on margin trading and derivatives. USDC, DAI, and ETH are all supported via the margin trading protocol. The company operates a spot DEX, which allows investors to trade these assets against the current bid–ask spread on the order book. The DEX employs a hybrid on–off chain strategy. Essentially, dYdX saves signed or pre-approved requests that have not yet been submitted to Ethereum. Cryptography is employed to ensure that these orders are only used to exchange funds for the desired item at the intended price. The DEX supports limit orders as well as a maximum slippage parameter for market orders in an effort to reduce slippage caused by price movements or front running.

dYdX provides the open-source software required to connect with the DEX to market makers and traders; alternatively, consumers can just use the user interface (UI). Having dYdX conduct the order matching adds a layer of trust because the infrastructure could be unavailable or not posting transactions for whatever reason. Allowing dYdX to match the orders poses little or no risk of the corporation stealing user funds because the signed orders can only be used as specified in the smart contract. When

Finally, the delegator has sole discretion in determining who is a qualified borrower and what contract terms are adequate. Credit delegation terms, for example, can be handled by a smart contract.

Alternatively, the delegated liquidity can be given to a smart contract, which can then use the liquidity to perform the required function. The fundamental advantage of credit delegation is that all loans in Aave are ultimately secured by collateral, regardless of who owns the asset.

To summarise, Aave goes above and beyond the loan options given by Compound and other competitors. Although not unique among competitors, Aave's flash loans provide additional income to investors, making it a tempting technique for providing liquidity. These utilities are also appealing to platform arbitrageurs and other applications that require instant liquidity for their use cases. Stable borrow rates are a critical innovation, and Aave is the only platform that now provides this service. This feature may be useful for larger players who cannot operate under the possible instability of fluctuating interest rates.

Derivatives

Yield Protocol

Yield Protocol presents a derivative model for zero-coupon secured bonds. The protocol specifies a yToken as an ERC-20 (fungible) token that settles in a defined quantity of a target asset at a given date. The contract will state that tokens with the same expiry date, target asset, collateral asset, and collateralization ratio are fungible. The tokens are collateralized by the collateral asset and have a needed maintenance collateralization ratio, similar to MakerDAO and other DeFi platforms we've explored. If the collateral's value falls below the required level of maintenance, the position can be liquidated by selling some or all of the collateral to cover the debt.

dYdX

dYdX is a firm that focuses on margin trading and derivatives. USDC, DAI, and ETH are all supported via the margin trading protocol. The company operates a spot DEX, which allows investors to trade these assets against the current bid–ask spread on the order book. The DEX employs a hybrid on–off chain strategy. Essentially, dYdX saves signed or pre-approved requests that have not yet been submitted to Ethereum. Cryptography is employed to ensure that these orders are only used to exchange funds for the desired item at the intended price. The DEX supports limit orders as well as a maximum slippage parameter for market orders in an effort to reduce slippage caused by price movements or front running.

dYdX provides the open-source software required to connect with the DEX to market makers and traders; alternatively, consumers can just use the user interface (UI). Having dYdX conduct the order matching adds a layer of trust because the infrastructure could be unavailable or not posting transactions for whatever reason. Allowing dYdX to match the orders poses little or no risk of the corporation stealing user funds because the signed orders can only be used as specified in the smart contract. When the orders match, they are sent to the Ethereum blockchain, where the smart contract helps with settlement.

In addition, an investor can use margined collateral to take a leveraged long or short position. The highest leverage allowed by dYdX is ten times. The positions can be isolated so that just one collateral deposit is used, or they can be cross-margined so that all of the investor's balances are pooled to serve as collateral. dYdX, like other protocols, has a maintenance margin requirement that, if not met, causes the collateral to be liquidated to close the position. External keepers who are paid to find and liquidate underwater holdings, similar to the MakerDAO method, can undertake the liquidations.

dYdX, like Compound and Aave, provides borrowing and lending. Flash loans are also available on the dYdX marketplaces. dYdX is a popular choice for DAI, ETH, and USDC flash liquidity since, unlike Aave, the flash loans are free. Given that flash loans are essentially risk-free in the realm of open smart contracts, it stands to reason that their interest rates would be driven to zero. Lending rates are defined by the duration of the loan and the relative risk of default. Repayment for flash loans is algorithmically enforced, and time is infinitesimal: only the user can make any function calls or transfers in a single transaction. While a specific user's transaction is in flight, no other Ethereum users can move funds or make any changes, resulting in no opportunity cost for the capital. As a result, a market participant giving free flash loans will, as expected, attract more users to their platform.

Flash loans, because they do not require any upfront cash, democratize access to funds for a variety of use cases. We demonstrated how flash loans can be used to refinance a loan in the Aave example. We will now demonstrate how to employ flash loans to take advantage of an arbitrage opportunity. The primary derivative product offered by dYdX is a BTC perpetual futures contract. Perpetual futures are a popular derivative product that is identical to ordinary futures but does not have a settlement date. The investor is essentially betting on the future price of an item by investing into a perpetual futures contract. The contract might be long or short, and it can include leverage or not. The Index Price of the perpetual futures contract is based on the average price of the underlying asset across the major exchanges.

The investor places margin collateral and decides on the direction and amount of leverage. Depending on whether more traders are long or short the underlying, in this case BTC, the contract might trade at a premium or discount to the Index Price.

The futures price is kept close to the Index by a financing rate paid from one side to the other. If the futures contract trades at a premium to the Index, the funding rate is positive, and longs pay shorts. The size of the funding rate is determined by the price difference relative to the Index. Similarly, if the contract is trading at a discount, the shorts compensate the longs. In order to keep the contract price near to the Index, the financing rate incentivizes investors to pick the other side from the majority. As long as the required margin is maintained, the investor can always close the trade at the difference in the notional position's price minus any negative amount kept on margin.

Synthetix

A decentralised alternative exists for many classic derivative products. DeFi, on the other hand, provides for new sorts of derivatives due to smart contracts. Synthetix is working on creating a new form of derivative.

Consider the creation of a derivative crypto asset, the value of which is predicated on an underlying asset that is neither owned nor escrowed. Synthetix is one company whose principal goal is to develop a wide range of liquid synthetic derivatives. At a high level, its model is simple and innovative. The company issues Synths, which are tokens backed by collateral and whose prices are tied to an underlying price feed. MakerDAO's DAI is a synthetic asset as well. Price feeds are provided via Chainlink's decentralised oracles. Theoretically, synths can track any asset, long or short, and even leveraged positions. In practice, no leverage is used, and the major assets tracked are cryptocurrencies, fiat currencies, and gold.

An sToken is a long Synth, such as a sUSD or a sBTC. The sUSD is a synthetic because its value is based on a price feed. An iToken is a short Synth, such as an iETH or an iMKR. Synthetix has its own platform token, SNX.

SNX is not a governance token like MKR or COMP, but rather a utility token or network token, which means it just allows you to use Synthetix capabilities. The unique collateral asset for the entire system is SNX.

When users mint Synths against their SNX, they incur debt in proportion to their total outstanding debt in USD. They become responsible for this percentage of the debt in the sense that they must return the total USD worth of their loan in order to unlock their SNX collateral. The worldwide debt of all Synths is thus collectively borne by Synth holders based on the USD-denominated percentage of debt they owned when they started their holdings. When the price of any Synth fluctuates, the total outstanding USD-denominated debt changes, and each holder stays responsible for the same percentage they were responsible for when they minted their Synths. As a result, when an SNX holder's Synths outperform the collective pool, the holder effectively gains, and vice versa, because their asset value (their Synth position) has surpassed debt growth (sum of all sUSD debt).

Tokenization

Tokenization is the process of taking an asset or bundle of assets, either on or off chain, and representing that asset on chain with potentially fractional ownership, or generating a composite token that holds a number of underlying tokens. A token can conform to several specifications depending on the type of features desired by the user. As previously stated, the most widely used token standard is ERC-20, often known as the fungible token standard. This interface defines abstractly how a token with non-unique and replaceable units (such as USD) should function. The ERC-721 standard, which defines non fungible tokens, is another option (NFTs). These tokens are one-of-a-kind, such as one indicating ownership of a work of fine art or a distinctive digital asset from a video game. DeFi applications can use these and other standards to support any token that uses the standard by just coding for the single standard.

Set Protocol

The "composite token" approach to tokenization is provided by Set Protocol. Set Protocol, rather than tokenizing assets that are not native to Ethereum, combines Ethereum tokens into composite tokens that act more like traditional exchange traded funds (ETFs). Set Protocol aggregates crypto assets into Sets, which are ERC-20 tokens that are fully collateralized by the components escrowed in a smart contract. A Set token can always be redeemed for its constituents. Based on the trading strategy, sets might be static or dynamic. Static Sets are simple to grasp and are just bundled tokens that the investor is interested in; the resulting Set can be transferred as a single unit.

Dynamic Sets define a trading strategy that determines when and how reallocations can be made. Some examples include "Moving Average" Sets, which switch between 100% ETH and 100% USDC anytime ETH crosses its X-day simple or exponentially weighted moving average.

These Set tokens, like traditional ETFs, contain fees and, in certain cases, performance-based incentives. The manager pre-programs the fees, which are paid directly to the management for that specific Set, when the Set is created. A buy fee (front-end load fee), a streaming fee (management fee), and a performance fee (percentage of profits above a high-water mark) are the various fee alternatives. The Set Protocol presently does not charge a fee, however this may change in the future.

Set Protocol's prices and returns are determined using MakerDAOs' publicly available oracle price feeds, which are also used by Synthetix. The primary benefit of dynamic Sets is that the trading strategies are openly written in a smart contract, allowing customers can see exactly how their funds are being allocated and simply redeem at any time.

Set Protocol also offers a Social Trading function, which allows a user to buy a Set whose portfolio is restricted to specific assets and whose reallocations are controlled by a single trader. These portfolios behave much more like mutual funds since they are actively managed. The advantages are similar in that the portfolio manager has a specified set of assets from which to choose, and the users benefit from the contract-enforced transparency.

wBTC

The wBTC application, designed for BTC, uses the representing off-chain assets on chain approach to tokenization. In general, wBTC permits BTC to be used as collateral or liquidity on all Ethereum-based DeFi services. Given that BTC has low volatility and is the most widely used cryptocurrency in terms of market capitalization, this trait opens up a vast potential cash pool for DeFi dApps.

Users, merchants, and custodians are the three main stakeholders in the wBTC ecosystem. Users are essentially the traders and DeFi participants who generate demand for the wBTC value proposition, namely, Ethereum-tokenized BTC. Users can buy wBTC from merchants by transferring BTC and completing the necessary KYC/AML procedures, making wBTC entry and exit points controlled and reliant on off-chain trust and infrastructure. Merchants are in charge of transmitting wBTC to custodians. At the point of transfer, the merchant notifies an on-chain Ethereum smart contract that the custodian has taken custody of the BTC and has been granted permission to mint wBTC. Custodians store BTC using industry-standard security techniques until it is removed from the wBTC ecosystem. Once the custodians have confirmed receipt, they can initiate wBTC minting, releasing wBTC to the merchant. Finally, the merchant closes the loop by transferring the wBTC to the user.

There is no single player who can control the minting and burning of wBTC, and all BTC entering the system is audited via transaction receipts that confirm possession of on-chain funds. These measures boost the system's openness and lower the system's inherent danger to users.

Because the network is made up of merchants and custodians, any fraud is rapidly removed from the network at a low overall cost compared to the expense incurred in a single centralised entity. A multi-signature wallet owned by the wBTC DAO is the mechanism by which merchants and custodians enter and exit the network. In this situation, the DAO lacks a governance token; instead, the DAO is controlled by a group of owners who can add and remove owners. The contract currently provides for a maximum of 50 owners, with a minimum of 11 to trigger a modification. If a certain number of criteria are met, the numbers 50 and 11 can be modified. This method is more centralised than the other governance techniques we've covered, but it's still more decentralised than having a single custodian oversee all of the wBTC.

Risks

As we have shown in earlier sections, DeFi enables developers to create new sorts of financial products and services, hence broadening the scope of financial technology. While DeFi can remove counterparty risk by eliminating middlemen and allowing financial assets to be exchanged in a trustless manner, the innovations, like any novel technology, present a new set of hazards. We must tackle these risks in order to provide users and institutions with a robust and fault-tolerant infrastructure capable of handling new financial applications at scale. DeFi will remain an exploratory technology without effective risk mitigation, limiting its use, adoption, and appeal.

DeFi is now facing smart contract, governance, Oracle, scaling, exchange, custodial, and regulatory issues.

Smart-Contract Risk

Crypto-focused products, especially exchanges, have been regularly hacked over the last decade. While many of these attacks occurred as a result of inadequate security practices, they highlight an important point: software is especially vulnerable to hacks and developer error. With their unique qualities, blockchains can eliminate traditional financial hazards such as counterparty risk, yet DeFi is built on code. This software base provides attackers with a broader attack surface than traditional financial institutions' danger vectors. As previously stated, public blockchains are open platforms. After the code is deployed, anyone can view and interact with it on a blockchain. Given that this programming is frequently in charge of keeping and moving blockchain native financial assets, it creates a new and distinct risk. Smart contract risk is the name given to this new attack vector.

So, what exactly does smart contract risk imply?

The cornerstone of DeFi is open computer code known as a smart contract. While Nick Szabo established the concept of a smart contract in his 1997 work, the implementation is new to popular technical practice. As a result, formal engineering approaches to assist limit the risk of smart contract defects and programming errors are still in the works. The recent DForce and bZx31 attacks illustrate the vulnerability of smart contract programming, and auditing firms such as Quantstamp, Trail of Bits, and Peckshield are emerging to fill this vacuum in best practices and smart contract expertise.

Smart Contract risk can take the form of a logical fault in the code or an economic exploit in which an attacker can remove funds from the platform in excess of the platform's intended capabilities. The latter can take the form of any common software flaw in the code. Assume we have a smart contract that is designed to escrow deposits from any user on a specific ERC-20 and transfer the entire balance to the winner of a lottery. The contract internally maintains track of how many tokens it has and uses that number as the amount when conducting the transfer. The bug will be included in our fictitious contract. Due to a rounding issue, the internal figure will be slightly greater than the actual amount of tokens held by the contract. When it tries to transfer, it transfers "too much," and the execution fails. If no failsafe was implemented, the tokens are functionally locked within the protocol. These are referred to colloquially as "bricked" funds since they cannot be recovered.

A more subtle economic exploitation would be preferable. There would be no clear breakdown in the logic of the code, but rather an opportunity for an economically equipped enemy to alter market conditions in such a way that an inappropriate profit might be made at the expense of the contract. Assume a contract serves as a conduit for the exchange of two tokens. It calculates the price by examining the exchange rate of another identical contract on the chain and offering that rate with a little tweak. It is worth noting that the other exchange is acting as a pricing oracle for this specific contract. When the oracle exchange has much less liquidity than the primary exchange in our scenario, the prospect of an economic exploit exists. A well-funded enemy can buy significantly on the oracle exchange to manipulate the price, then buy even more on the primary exchange in the opposite direction to profit from the price fluctuation.

As a result of manipulating a low liquidity oracle, the attacker was able to create a reduced pricing on a high liquidity exchange.

Economic exploitation becomes much more difficult when you realise that flash loans essentially allow any Ethereum user to become financially prepared for a single transaction. When creating protocols, special attention must be taken to ensure that they cannot be exploited by huge market volatility during a single transaction. A flash attack is an economic exploit that makes use of a flash loan. In February 2020, a series of high-profile flash attacks were carried out on bZx Fulcrum, a loan market similar to Compound. The attacker obtained a flash loan and used some of the funds to purchase a leveraged short position, while the remaining was used to manipulate the price of the oracle exchange on which the short position was based. The attacker then profitably closed the short, unwound the market trade, and repaid the flash loan. The net profit was about $300,000 in money previously held by bZx, with a near-zero upfront investment.

Governance Risk

Risks in programming are nothing new. They have, in fact, been there since the start of modern computing more than a half-century ago. Because the application is autonomous and regulated by smart contracts, programming risk is the only concern to some protocols, such as Uniswap. Other DeFi applications rely on more than merely self-replicating computer code. MakerDAO, the previously stated decentralised credit facility, is reliant on a human-controlled governance process that actively alters protocol parameters to keep the system solvent. Many other DeFi protocols rely on similar mechanisms and humans to actively minimise protocol risk. This introduces a new risk, governance risk, to the DeFi ecosystem. Protocol governance refers to the representative or liquid democratic systems that allow protocol alterations. To participate in the governance process, users and investors must purchase a token on a liquid marketplace that has been explicitly allocated protocol governance powers. Holders of these tokens can use them to vote on protocol improvements and help shape the future. Governance tokens often have a set quantity, which aids in opposing attempts by anyone to obtain a majority (51 percent), but they expose the protocol to the possibility of control by a bad actor.

While we have yet to witness a serious governance attack in action, new projects such as Automata38 allow users to directly purchase governance votes, which will certainly accelerate the prospect of malicious/hostile governance. Traditional fintech companies are frequently controlled by the founders, which lessens the danger of an external party influencing or changing the company's direction or product. DeFi protocols, on the other hand, are subject to assault as soon as the governance system is activated. Any financially capable adversary can simply obtain a majority of liquid governance tokens to assume control of the protocol and steal cash.

On March 13, 2021, True Seigniorage Dollar was subjected to a governance attack. In this particular case, the developers held only 9 percent of the DAO. The attacker steadily purchased $TSD until he owned 33% of the DAO. The hacker then presented and voted on an implementation. The attacker introduced code that allowed him to manufacture 11.5 quintillion $TSD and subsequently sell 11.8 billion $TSD tokens on Pancakeswap. We have yet to witness a successful governance attack on any Ethereum-based DeFi project, but there is no doubt that a well-funded adversary will eventually attack a protocol if the potential benefit outweighs the cost of attack.

Oracle Risk

Oracles are one of the final unsolved challenges in DeFi, and most DeFi protocols require them to function properly. Oracles, at their core, seek to address a basic question: How can off-chain data be securely reported on chain? Blockchains are totally self-contained and have no awareness of the outside world other than the transactions added to the native blockchain in the absence of oracles. Many DeFi systems require safe, tamper-resistant asset pricing to ensure that routine procedures like liquidations and prediction market resolutions work properly. The dependency of the protocol on these data flows creates Oracle risk.

Oracles pose major hazards to the systems they assist in supporting. If an oracle's Cost of Corruption ever falls below an attacker's potential Profit from Corruption, the oracle is extremely vulnerable to attack.

Three types of Oracle solutions have been created, developed, and used to date. The first type of oracle is a Schelling-point oracle. This oracle relies on token holders to vote on the outcome of an event or report the price of an asset. Augur and UMA are two examples of this type of oracle. While Schelling-point oracles maintain the decentralised components of protocols that rely on them, they have long resolution times.

The API oracle is the second sort of Oracle solution. These oracles are centralised entities that respond asynchronously to data or price queries. Provable, Oraclize, and Chainlink are a few examples. All systems that rely on API-based Oracles must have confidence in the data provider's ability to answer appropriately to all queries.

A tailored, application-specific oracle service is the third form of oracle. Maker and Compound both employ this form of oracle. Its design varies depending on the protocol for which it was created. Compound, for example, relies on a single data provider controlled by the Compound team to give all on-chain price data to the Compound oracle.

Oracles, as they currently exist, pose the greatest risk to DeFi protocols that rely on them. All on-chain oracles are subject to front-running, and arbitrageurs have cost millions of dollars. Furthermore, oracle systems such as Chainlink and Maker have had devastating outages with disastrous consequences.

Scaling Risk

As previously stated, the block size of Ethereum and other "Proof of Work" (the consensus process) blockchains is set. Every Ethereum miner must execute all of the included transactions on their equipment for a block to become part of the chain. It is impractical to expect each miner to conduct all financial transactions for a global financial market. Ethereum currently has a maximum TPS of 15 TPS. Nonetheless, practically all of DeFi today is stored on this blockchain. In comparison to Visa, which can process up to 65,000 transactions per second, Ethereum can manage less than 0.1 percent of the throughput. DeFi is at risk of not being able to meet demand due to Ethereum's lack of scalability.

Much work is being put into expanding Ethereum's scalability or replacing Ethereum with an alternative blockchain that can manage bigger transaction volumes more easily. To yet, all efforts for Ethereum have been futile. However, new platforms such as Polkadot, Zilliqa, and Algorand provide some solutions to this scaling problem. A new consensus algorithm, Proof of Stake, is one actively pursued solution to the problem. Proof of Stake simply substitutes staking an asset on the next block for mining (which involves a probabilistic wait time), with majority rules identical to PoW.

Staking, a key notion in cryptocurrencies and DeFi, refers to a user escrowing funds in a smart contract and being penalised (losing cash) if they stray from expected behavior. Voting for numerous candidate blocks is an example of harmful activity in Proof of Stake.

This behavior demonstrates a lack of discernment and skews voting figures, and it is thus sanctioned. Proof of Stake security is built on the idea that a malicious actor would have to amass more of the staked asset (ether in the case of Ethereum) than the whole staker community on that chain. This goal is infeasible, resulting in strong security features akin to PoW.

Vertical and horizontal scaling are two other general methods for enhancing blockchain throughput. Vertical scaling focuses all transaction processing on a single huge processor. This centralization decreases the communication overhead (transaction/block latency) associated with a

PoW blockchain like Ethereum, but it results in a centralised architecture in which one machine handles the majority of the system's operations. Some blockchains, like Solana, take this strategy and can achieve up to 50,000 TPS.

Horizontal scaling, on the other hand, divides the system's work into several sections, keeping decentralisation while boosting the system's throughput through parallelization. This strategy (known as sharding) is used by Ethereum 2.0 in conjunction with a Proof of Stake consensus algorithm.

The technological architecture40 of Ethereum 2.0 differs significantly from that of vertically scaled blockchains like as Solana, but the benefits are the same. Ethereum 2.0 employs horizontal scalability with several blockchains to achieve transaction rates of up to 50,000 per second.

The construction of Ethereum 2.0 has been postponed for several years, but its mainnet, which will have a basic blockchain without smart contract capabilities, is expected to go operational in 2021. The functional specification for transmitting transactions between Ethereum 2.0's horizontally scaled blockchains has not yet been finalised.

The Ethereum layer-2 landscape is another competitor with the ability to lessen scaling risk. A layer 2 solution is one that is built on top of a blockchain and depends on cryptography and economic guarantees to maintain desired levels of security. Transactions can be signed and aggregated in a way that makes them resistant to malicious actors, but they are not directly recorded to the blockchain until there is some kind of disagreement. This eliminates the limitations of a set block size and block rate, allowing for significantly faster throughput. Some layer-2 solutions are now operational.

Layer-2 utilisation has remained stable while Ethereum's transaction fees have reached new highs. The space has been slowly evolving, and many active solutions do not enable smart contracts or decentralised exchanges. An Optimistic Rollup is one approach in the works. An optimistic rollup is a procedure that aggregates transactions off-chain into a single digest that is published to the chain at regular intervals. These summaries can only be combined and submitted by an aggregator who has a bond (stake). Importantly, the state is presumed to be correct unless challenged. If a challenge is issued, cryptography can demonstrate if the aggregator posted an incorrect state. As an incentive, the prover is subsequently compensated with a percentage of the malicious aggregator's bond (similar to a Keeper mechanism). Optimistic rollups have yet to offer working main nets, necessitating costly fraud proofs as well as frequent rollup transaction posting, reducing throughput and raising average transaction costs. Many initiatives seek to reduce the scalability concerns that DeFi faces today, but there is no obvious winner. As long as blockchain scaling limits DeFi's growth, applications' potential influence will be constrained.

DEX Risk

Today's most popular DeFi products are similar to those seen in traditional finance. DeFi is mostly used for increasing leverage, trading, and acquiring exposure to synthetic assets. Trading, as expected, accounts for the majority of on-chain activity, but the emergence of new assets (ERC-20 tokens, Synthetics, and so on) has resulted in a Cambrian explosion in DEXs. The design and architecture of these decentralised exchanges differ greatly, but they all seek to answer the same problem: how to construct the greatest decentralised venue for asset exchange?

The Ethereum DEX scene is dominated by two types: Automated Market Makers (AMMs) and order-book exchanges. Both forms of DEXs differ in architecture and risk characteristics. AMMs, on the other hand, are the most popular DEX to date since they enable users to exchange assets in a trustless and safe manner while eliminating traditional counterparty risk. AMMs provide users with rapid access to quotes on an exchange pair by keeping exchange liquidity in a trustless smart contract. Perhaps the most well-known example of an AMM, also known as a Constant-Function Market Maker, is Uniswap (CFMM).

Today's most popular DeFi products are similar to those seen in traditional finance. DeFi is mostly used for increasing leverage, trading, and acquiring exposure to synthetic assets. Trading, as expected, accounts for the majority of on-chain activity, but the emergence of new assets (ERC-20 tokens, Synthetics, and so on) has resulted in a Cambrian explosion in DEXs. The design and architecture of these decentralised exchanges differ greatly, but they all seek to answer the same problem: how to construct the greatest decentralised venue for asset exchange?

The Ethereum DEX scene is dominated by two types: Automated Market Makers (AMMs) and order-book exchanges. Both forms of DEXs differ in architecture and risk characteristics.

AMMs are the most popular DEX to date since they enable users to exchange assets in a trustless and safe manner while eliminating traditional counterparty risk. AMMs provide users with rapid access to quotes on an exchange pair by keeping exchange liquidity in a trustless smart contract.

Perhaps the most well-known example of an AMM, also known as a Constant-Function Market Maker, is Uniswap (CFMM). On-chain order-book DEXs face a distinct but common set of risks. These exchanges suffer from the underlying blockchain's scalability concerns, and are frequently prone to front running by clever arbitrage bots. Because of the prevalence of low-sophistication market makers, order-book DEXs frequently have wide spreads. Traditional finance can rely on sophisticated market makers such as Jump, Virtu, DRW, Jane Street, and others, whereas order-book DEXs are frequently obliged to rely on a single market maker for each asset pair.

This reliance stems from the DeFi market's infancy, as well as the complicated computing infrastructure required to supply on-chain liquidity to order-book DEXs. We expect these barriers to fall as the market evolves and more traditional market makers to enter the ecosystem; for the time being, however, these obstacles represent a major barrier to entry. In any case, both AMM and order-book DEXs can minimise counterparty risk while also providing traders with a noncustodial and trustless exchange platform.

Several decentralised exchanges use a totally off-chain order book, keeping the benefits of a noncustodial DEX but avoiding the market making and scaling issues that on-chain order-book DEXs provide. These exchanges work by settling all position entries and exits on chain while keeping a totally off-chain limit-order book. This allows the DEX to sidestep the scale and UX challenges that on-chain order-book DEXs encounter, but it also introduces a new set of issues related to regulatory compliance.

Although hazards exist in the DEX ecosystem today, they should diminish over time as technology progresses and market participants become more sophisticated.

Custodial Risk

There are three types of custody: sole custody, joint custody, and third-party custody. With self-custody, the user creates their own solution, which could be a flash drive that is not connected to the internet, a hard copy, or a vaulting device. There is a combination of self-custody and an external remedy in partial custody (e.g., Bitgo). In this case, a hack on the external provider yields insufficient data to reconstruct the private key. However, if the user loses their private key, they can rebuild it using the external solution. Third-party custody is the final option. Many organizations that formerly concentrated on custody in centralised finance are now offering solutions in decentralised finance (e.g., Fidelity Digital Assets).

In general, retail investors have two choices. The first option is self-custody, in which users have complete authority over their keys. This comprises a hardware wallet, a web wallet (like as MetaMask, which stores keys in a browser), a desktop wallet, and even a paper wallet. The second type of wallet is a custodial wallet. Your private keys are kept here by a third party. Coinbase and Binance are two examples.

The most obvious risk of self-custody is the loss or locking of private keys. The New York Times published a story in January 2021 about a programmer who used a hardware wallet but forgot the password. 42 The wallet has $220 million in bitcoin. The hardware wallet permits 10 password attempts before erasing all data. The coder has only two attempts left.

Risks are also associated with delegated custody. For example, if your private keys are stored on an exchange, the exchange could be hacked and your keys lost. The majority of exchanges maintain the majority of private keys in "cold storage" (on a drive not connected to the internet). Nonetheless, there is a lengthy history of exchange hacks, such as Mt Gox (2011-2014) 850,000 bitcoin, Bitfloor (2012) 24,000 bitcoin, Bitfinex (2016) 120,000 bitcoin, Coincheck (2018) 523 million NEM worth $500 million at the time, and Binance (2019) 7,000 bitcoin. The frequency of the attacks has decreased. Some exchangers, like Coinbase, even provide insurance. All of these attacks were launched against centralised exchanges. We've already gone over some of the attacks on DEXs.

Regulatory Risk

As the DeFi market grows in size and importance, it will be subjected to increased regulatory scrutiny. The CFTC has lately ordered major centralised spot and futures exchanges to comply with KYC/AML compliance directives, and DEXs appear to be next. Several decentralised derivatives exchanges, such as dYdX, are already required to geoblock US consumers from accessing certain exchange services. While the noncustodial and decentralised structure of DEXs creates a legal grey area with an unknown regulatory future, there is little doubt that regulation will be implemented as the industry grows. Due to legal issues, a well-known algorithmic Stablecoin project known as Basis was forced to suspend down in December of 2018. For future comparable startups, a sobering statement remains on their home page: "Unfortunately, having to apply US securities regulation to the system had a severe negative impact on our ability to launch Basis [...] As a result, I am sorry to inform you that we have decided to return funds to our investors. Unfortunately, this also means that the Basis project will be terminated."

DeFi has seen an increase in the number of anonymous protocol founders in response to regulatory pressure. An unidentified team forked the original Basis project earlier this year. Governance tokens, which have been published by many DeFi projects, are also coming under more attention as the SEC continues to determine if these new assets will be regulated as securities. Compound, Ethereum's decentralised money market, just issued a governance token with no intrinsic value or rights to future cash flows. As a result, Compound was able to sidestep SEC securities regulation, freeing the company from security issuance requirements. We anticipate that more projects will follow Compound's lead in the future, and that most will exercise prudence before issuing additional coins; many projects learned from the hefty penalties imposed by the SEC following the 2017 ICO bubble.

The CFTC has concluded that many significant market-cap cryptocurrencies are commodities, exempting them from money-transmitter restrictions. Individual states, such as New York, have enacted legislation aimed at brokerages that facilitate the transfer and exchange of cryptocurrencies. As DeFi grows and the overall number of issued assets grows, we anticipate to see more detailed and nuanced regulation focused at DeFi protocols and their users.

From a regulatory aspect, cryptocurrency taxes have yet to be completely defined, and accounting software/on-chain monitoring is only now beginning to reach mass retail consumers. For example, as of December 31, 2020, the IRS draught proposal requires reporting on form 1040 of: any free receipt of cryptocurrency, including airdrops and hard forks; exchange of cryptocurrency for goods or services; purchase or sale of cryptocurrency; exchange of virtual currency for other property, including another virtual currency; and acquisition or disposition of a financial interest in a cryptocurrency. It is not possible to transfer virtual currency from one wallet to another. The requirements also provide that if you received cryptocurrencies for employment, you must disclose it on form W2.45. While the DeFi regulatory landscape is being aggressively examined, with new regulatory decisions such as permitting banks to store bitcoin being made on a daily basis, the market outlook is murky, with many existing challenges needing to be navigated.

DeFi service categories

Due to their programmability and composability, the possible configurations of DeFi services are nearly endless. However, certain core functions, analogous to those in centralized finance, can be identified. These labels are generic and not intended as regulatory classifications for jurisdictions in which the terms used have legal import.

Stablecoins seek to maintain a constant value for tokens relative to some stable asset – most commonly the US dollar. The ability to avoid the volatility of non-stabilized cryptocurrency such as bitcoin and ether is one reason for the growth in DeFi. Custodial Stablecoins use holdings of fiat currency or high-quality liquid assets as a reserve. Though they may be used in DeFi, these Stablecoins are not DeFi services themselves because they involve centralized trust and custody

Exchanges allow customers to trade one digital asset for another. The assets involved may be Stablecoins or floating-value tokens.

Unlike centralized exchanges such as Coinbase or Binance, decentralized exchange (DEX) protocols are DeFi services because they do not take custody of user funds and may not control other aspects of the process such as order book management and matching. An important category of DEX protocols for DeFi are automated market-makers (AMM), where an algorithm continuously prices transactions based on orders and available liquidity, rather than matching through an order book.

Credit involves the creation of interest-bearing instruments that must be repaid at maturity. It is based on a mutual relationship of borrowers and lenders, which can be either bilateral (peer-to-peer) or based on pooled capital. Credit terms can be quite complex, and these instruments can themselves be securitized and traded. DeFi borrowing and lending replaces the intermediating function of financial service providers with automated, decentralized, non-custodial protocols. While the lack of credit ratings and legal recourse means that digital asset loans are nearly always over-collateralized, DeFi also allows for uncollateralized flash loans in which assets are borrowed and repaid (with interest) within the span of a single block's time.

Derivatives create synthetic financial assets whose value is reliant upon or derived from an underlying asset or group of assets. Common financial derivatives include futures and options, which pay out based on the value of an asset at some time in the future or deliver the underlying asset. DeFi derivatives can be programmed and composed into virtually any configuration. For example, a derivative could create a synthetic asset that behaves as a stock, commodity, swap or another digital asset. It could involve a non-fungible token (NFT) uniquely associated with an art or real estate asset. It might be tied to the activity of a business, creating a crowdfunding service. Or the value could be tied to a future real-world event, such as the outcome of a sporting event or political campaign, turning the derivatives exchange into a prediction market. Prediction markets may also incentivize decentralized information generation or dispute resolution through the wisdom of crowds.

Insurance pools risk by trading the payment of a guaranteed small premium for the possibility of collecting a large payout in the event of a covered scenario. In DeFi insurance, decentralized transactional and governance systems are used to manage and structure the insurance life cycle for certain types of risks such as smart contract hacks. Though technically insurance contracts are derivatives – they pay out based on some external event – insurance plays a distinctive risk-hedging function in markets by spreading risks across a common capital pool

Asset management involves the oversight of financial assets for others and seeks to maximize the value of the whole portfolio based on risk preferences, time horizons or other conditions. DeFi asset management promises greater transparency and efficiency in constructing and executing investment strategies, by incorporating the asset management life cycle into a DApp.

PROBLEMS DeFi SOLVES

Inefficiency

Inefficiency is the first of traditional finance's five weaknesses. DeFi can complete financial transactions with high asset volumes and little friction, which would normally be a significant organizational load for traditional finance. DeFi develops reusable smart contracts in the form of dApps that perform a specific financial transaction. These dApps are open to any user who desires that specific type of service, such as executing a put option, regardless of transaction size. Within the parameters of the smart contract and the blockchain on which the application runs, a user can mainly self-serve. In the case of Ethereum-based DeFi, anyone who pays the fixed gas charge, which is normally approximately $15.00 for a transfer and $25.00 for a dApp functionality like leveraging against collateral, can access the contracts. Once in place, these contracts continue to supply services with almost no organizational overhead.

Keepers are external players who are directly compensated for providing a service to DeFi protocols, such as monitoring positions to ensure that they are adequately collateralized or triggering state updates for various functions. Keeper rewards are frequently organized as an auction to guarantee that a dApp's advantages and services are optimally priced. Pure, open competition adds value to DeFi platforms by ensuring that customers pay market prices for the services they require. A fork is another concept that encourages efficiency. A fork is a duplicate and reuse of code with upgrades or enhancements added on top in the context of open source programming. The use of two parallel currencies and chains is a common split of blockchain systems. This encourages protocol competition and the development of the greatest possible smart contract platform.

Not only is the code of the entire Ethereum blockchain public and forkable, but so is the code of any DeFi dApp built on top of Ethereum. If there are any inefficient or suboptimal DeFi apps, the code may be quickly copied, improved, and redeployed by forking. The open nature of DeFi and blockchains lends itself to forking and its benefits.

Forking introduces a novel challenge to DeFi platforms, namely vampirism. Vampirism is a carbon copy or near-carbon replica of a DeFi platform that is aimed to capture liquidity or users by offering more incentives than the platform it is copying. The greater incentives are usually in the form of inflationary awards that are delivered at a much higher rate than the original platform. Users may be drawn to the bigger possible payout for the same capability, resulting in a decrease in use and liquidity on the first platform.

If the inflationary rewards are flawed, the clone may collapse after a large asset bubble in the long run. Clones could also select models that are closer to optimal and replace the original platform. Vampirism is not an inherent risk or fault, but rather a complicating aspect resulting from DeFi's openness and competition. The selecting process will eventually result in more robust financial infrastructure that is more efficient.

Limited Access

As smart contract platforms evolve to more scalable implementations, user friction decreases, enabling a broader spectrum of users and therefore mitigating traditional finance's second flaw: limited access.

DeFi provides direct access to financial services to huge underserved groups, such as the worldwide unbanked population and small enterprises that employ significant percentages of the workforce (for example, roughly 50 percent in the United States). The overall impact on the global economy should be extremely beneficial. Even customers who have access to traditional financial services, such as bank accounts, mortgages, and credit cards, do not have access to the most competitive pricing and advantageous conditions; these products and structures are reserved to huge institutions. DeFi provides access to the full financial infrastructure to any user, regardless of wealth or geographic location. Yield farming gives many people access to financial services who would otherwise be excluded by regular finance. In short, yield farming compensates users for staking capital or following a protocol with inflationary or contract-funded payments. These benefits can be paid out in the same underlying asset that the user owns or in a separate asset, such as a governance token.

Yield farming is open to all users. A user can wager any amount, no matter how tiny, and receive a proportional payout. This capacity is especially useful in the case of governance tokens. Through the issued token, a user of a protocol that issues a governance token via yield farming becomes a partial owner of the platform. This technique, which is uncommon in traditional banking, is a widespread and celebrated manner of giving ownership of the platform to the people who use and benefit from it.

A fascinating side effect of yield farming is that a user can build an Initial DeFi Offering (IDO) by creating his own Uniswap trading pair. By becoming the first liquidity provider on the pair, the user can establish the first exchange rate. Assume the user's token is known as DFT and has a total supply of 2 million. By starting the market with 1 million DFT and 100,000 USDC, the user can make each DFT worth 0.10 USDC. DFT can be purchased by any ERC-20 token holder, driving up the price. The user obtains all trading fees as the sole liquidity source. As a result, the user is able to gain rapid access to as many users as possible. If the user controls the supply outside of the quantity delivered to the Uniswap market, the strategy creates an artificial price floor for the token and, as a result, hampers price discovery. An IDO's trade-offs should be considered as an alternative, or strategy, for a user's token distribution. IDOs democratize DeFi access in two ways. For starters, an IDO allows a project to list on high-traffic DeFi exchanges with no entrance restrictions other than the initial money. Second, an IDO gives a user fast access to the best new projects following the project lists.

Opacity

The third disadvantage of traditional finance is its obscurity. DeFi solves this problem neatly through the open and contractual nature of agreements. In terms of transparency, smart contracts provide an instant benefit. All parties are aware of their counterparts' capitalization and, to the extent necessary, can observe how money will be used. The parties can examine the contracts to see if the terms are agreeable in order to eliminate any uncertainty about what will happen when they interact under the contract conditions.

This transparency significantly reduces the possibility of legal obligations and provides peace of mind to smaller participants who, in the existing atmosphere of traditional banking, could be exploited by larger counterparties by delaying or even withholding their share of a financial arrangement. Realistically, the average user does not grasp the contract code, but can feel secure because of the platform's open-source nature and the knowledge of the crowd. Overall, DeFi reduces counterparty risk, resulting in a slew of efficiencies not found in traditional finance. Participants in DeFi are responsible for adhering to the conditions of the contracts they use. Staking is one strategy for enforcing appropriate behavior. Staking is the process of escrowing a cryptocurrency into a contract, with the contract releasing the cryptocurrency to the proper counterparty only once the contract terms are completed; otherwise, the asset reverts to the original holder. Parties may be compelled to stake their claims or interactions. Staking is a method of enforcing agreements by imposing a monetary penalty on the misbehaving party and a monetary reward on the counterparty. The physical incentive should be as good as, if not better than, the outcome of the original contract terms. These open incentive systems give far more secure and visible guarantees than typical financial contracts.

A token contract is another sort of smart contract in DeFi that promotes transparency. Tokenization enables a system's ownership and economics to be transparent. Users may see the precise number of tokens in the system as well as the inflation and deflation characteristics.

Centralized Control

The fault in traditional finance is the strong control exercised by governments and huge institutions, which have a virtual monopoly on elements such as the money supply, inflation rate, and access to the best investment possibilities. DeFi challenges this centralised control by delegating authority to open protocols with transparent and immutable attributes. A parameter of a DeFi dApp, such as the inflation rate, can be controlled by the community of stakeholders or even a programmed algorithm. If a dApp contains administrator-only privileges, all users are aware of the privileges, and any user can easily construct a less-centralized counterpart.

Because of blockchain's open-source culture and the public nature of all smart contracts, defects and inefficiencies in a DeFi project can be easily recognised and "forked away" by users who copy and fix the problematic project. As a result, DeFi tries to create protocols that naturally and elegantly encourage stakeholders while maintaining a healthy balance through rigorous mechanism design. There are, of course, trade-offs between having a centralised party and not having one. In a crisis, centralised authority allows for radically decisive action, which is sometimes required but may also be an overreaction. The route to decentralising finance will undoubtedly be fraught with growing pains due to the difficulties in anticipating every eventuality and economic detail. However, the openness and security achieved through a decentralised method will ultimately result in strong robust protocols that can become trusted financial infrastructure for a worldwide user base. The rules of functioning of a decentralised autonomous organization (DAO) are written in smart contracts, which specify who can execute what behavior or upgrade. A governance token, which grants an owner a percentage of the vote on future outcomes, is prevalent in a DAO.

Lack of Interoperability

Traditional financial products are difficult to connect with one another, requiring at least a wire transfer and, in many circumstances, cannot be recombined. DeFi has a lot of potential, and new improvements are coming at a non-linear rate. This expansion is being spurred by the simplicity with which DeFi products can be combined. Once some basic infrastructure has been established, for example, to generate a synthetic asset, any new protocols allowing for borrowing and lending can be implemented. A higher layer would enable leverage to be achieved on top of borrowed assets. As new platforms emerge, such composability can expand in an ever-increasing variety of directions. As a result, DeFi Legos is a popular analogy for describing the process of combining existing protocols to create a new protocol. We shall highlight a few benefits of this composability below, especially tokenization and networked liquidity. Tokenization is a fundamental component of DeFi platform integration. Consider a portion of ownership in a private commercial real estate venture. It would be impossible in traditional finance to use this asset as security for a loan or as margin to initiate a levered derivative position. Because DeFi is based on shared interfaces, apps can easily plug into one another's assets, repackage, and subdivide positions as needed. Through tokenization, DeFi has the potential to increase liquidity in historically illiquid assets. Making fractional shares from a unitary asset, such as a stock, is a straightforward use case. This approach can be extended to provide partial ownership of scarce resources such as rare paintings. Tokens can be used as collateral for any other DeFi service, including leverage and derivatives.

We may flip this paradigm and construct token bundles of groups of real-world or digital assets that can be traded like an ETF. Consider a dApp that is comparable to a real estate investment trust (REIT), but with the extra capability of allowing the owner to subdivide the REIT into individual real estate components in order to determine a desired geographic distribution and allocation within the REIT.

Ownership of the token gives you direct control over the distribution of the properties. To liquidate the stake, the owner might trade the token on a decentralised exchange.

Tokenizing hard assets, like as real estate or precious metals, is more challenging than tokenizing digital assets because hard assets practical considerations, such as upkeep and storage, cannot be imposed by code. Legal constraints between jurisdictions are also a hurdle for tokenization; yet, the benefit of safe, contractual tokenization for the majority of use cases should not be underestimated. In a DeFi platform, a tokenized version of a position is a pluggable derivative asset that may be used in another platform.

Tokenization makes it possible for the benefits and characteristics of one position to be transferrable to another. Compound enables robust lending markets in which a position can earn variable-rate interest priced in a specific token, and the position itself is a token. If the underlying asset is ETH, for example, the ETH deposit wrapper known as cETH (cToken) can be used in place of the base asset. As a result, an ETH-backed derivative is created that also earns variable-rate interest according to the Compound protocol. Tokenization thus opens up new revenue models for dApps by allowing them to integrate asset holdings directly into Compound or use the cToken interface to benefit from Compound's interest rates.

In the exchange use case, the concept of interoperability simply extends to liquidity. Traditional exchanges, particularly those used by ordinary investors, are unable to easily share liquidity with other exchanges without special access to a prime broker, which is often restricted to hedge funds. In DeFi, any exchange application can leverage the liquidity and rates of any other exchange on the same blockchain as a subcomponent of the contract. This capability enables networked liquidity, resulting in extremely competitive pricing for users within the same application.

Risks associated with DeFi

Financial

Market risk is the possibility that asset value will decline over some time horizon due to market conditions, new information or traders' idiosyncratic behavior. Though it may not be the role of governments to protect against market risk for well-informed and well-capitalized investors in a well-functioning market, it is appropriate for them to be concerned that those conditions are met. For DeFi, regulatory classifications will define whether requirements designed to prevent undue market risk – such as disclosure obligations and accredited investor standards – are applicable. DeFi's novelty, as well as the ease of transferring funds and creating complex instruments, may increase the possibility of abuses, whether by the creators of DeFi protocols, the operators of exchanges or third-party manipulators. At the same time, policy-makers may want to consider the implications of potential increases in transparency as well as the retention of asset custody. There may also be a lack of observability and standardized price-discovery mechanisms found in digital asset markets. The inability to compare many of the current tokens to any fundamentals is a driver of big swings in valuation and overall volatility.

Counterparty risk is the possibility that a counterparty will default on its obligations to a financial instrument. This might involve failing to repay a loan (credit risk) or failing to settle a transaction by providing the specified asset (settlement risk). Though some credit risk is mitigated through interest rates for loans, it might be a particular problem in DeFi, where the volatility of underlying digital assets produces under collateralization, the ease of credit creation leads to excessive leverage, or the algorithmic determination of interest produces inaccuracies. The lack of fixed identities in a pseudonymous network presents additional challenges in terms of determining creditworthiness. DeFi attempts to account for this through over-collateralization requirements. Some traditional settlement risks are not present in DeFi because there is no separate settlement step; transactions are executed through transfer of the underlying value on the blockchain – but only if both sides of the transaction are operating on the same chain. Moreover, given the rapid inflow of capital, there are strong incentives and many opportunities for scams.

Users may not receive the assets they anticipate due to fraud, especially when information asymmetries limit their understanding of investment decisions or the code that governs transaction execution.

Liquidity risk is the possibility that there will be insufficient funds or assets available to realize the value of a financial asset. Failure of liquidity for a borrower or trader (such as a short seller) means the position is involuntarily liquidated and the available assets allocated to owners or creditors. Insufficient liquidity also magnifies market inefficiencies, such as price movements resulting from trades. DeFi liquidation processes differ from traditional instruments, where a centralized counterparty (a bank, the International Swaps and Derivates Association, a clearing house, etc.) executes the process. DeFi services often incentivize market makers to liquidate under-collateralized loans, performing a function analogous to a foreclosure auction for real estate. If the liquidation incentive structures fail, however, original counterparties and liquidity providers hold unanticipated default risk. In DeFi markets where most transactions are automated and available continuously, the speed of liquidations may preclude rational decision making. On centralized exchanges, cascades of automated liquidations have on several occasions produced "flash crashes", where prices dropped precipitously and trading was taken offline until the market settled. Such last-resort remedies may not be available for decentralized services.

DeFi liquidity risks may be mitigated through governance logic and the careful design of incentive structures. Game-theoretic analysis must anticipate not only expected behaviors, but other profitable strategies. For example, a market participant could deliberately skew liquidity in certain DeFi services and bet against the arbitrary results. Systems designed to incentivize stable liquidity could limit this risk. Because financial risks arise from profit seeking, constant vigilance is needed to address new strategies. Flash loans create a unique set of risks. They may effectively create artificial liquidity for a short period of time, seemingly addressing both counterparty and liquidity risk.

If the loan cannot be paid back in time, the original transaction is never incorporated into the block and the loan is essentially rolled back before issuance. While flash loans may be used as near risk-free and low-cost capital for legitimate arbitrage transactions, they can also be employed in attacks.

The temporary surge of funds can be used to manipulate prices and force artificial liquidation, often through the interaction of multiple DeFi services. Several million dollars have been stolen through several such high-profile, near-instantaneous attacks.

Technical

half of digital asset hacks in 2020 targeted DeFi services, up from a negligible number in 2019 – a trend likely to continue as the value of assets involved grows. While the largest public blockchain networks, such as Bitcoin and Ethereum, have avoided significant breaches, blockchain-based DApps and the centralized exchanges or wallets handling funds have proven far less secure. The technical complexity and immaturity of the DeFi market increases the likelihood of significant vulnerabilities, with the vast majority created in the past few years. The degree of interconnection among DeFi protocols may also expand the attack surface available to malicious actors. Services aim to police market abuses through radical transparency and trust minimization rather than centralized oversight. Some include sophisticated, multilayered incentive structures to discourage attacks, in addition to technical measures for security and market integrity. Some have used their decentralized governance mechanisms to implement changes in response to failures or potential scenarios identified by the community. These measures are not foolproof. If DeFi continues to grow and attract less sophisticated market participants, investor protection concerns may grow

Transaction risks are limitations or failures of the underlying blockchain network. If the base-layer settlement network is successfully attacked, allows for double-spending, becomes too expensive for transactions or lacks the necessary throughput, those failures will affect the application layer.

The long-planned upgrade to Eth2 (Ethereum version 2.0), which aims for significant performance improvements, thus represents an important development for DeFi. This upgrade will also shift Ethereum to proof-of-stake consensus, which does not require the intensive energy usage of proof-of-work mining.

Smart contract risks deal with code that does not execute as intended. All software has the potential for bugs. A programming flaw can cause a smart contract to fail to perform as desired, or attackers can exploit vulnerabilities to drain funds or engage in malicious activities. For example, where code has not been written properly, it can allow for exploits such as reentrancy attacks. Complex software performing novel functions in a relatively untested environment, and often written by teams lacking the expertise or inclination to employ the most robust development practices, will tend to have more bugs than the norm.29 Even without attacks, the smart contract might not accurately reflect the understanding of all parties. Because DeFi software is automated financial services, rather than a recordkeeping mechanism subject to human override, coding errors can lead directly to financial losses, often without easy redress.

Moreover, transparency of code has two sides – the visibility may make smart contracts more vulnerable to exploits or may offer opportunities for white hat hackers and bounty hunters to increase the robustness of the code. Mechanisms such as security audits and bug bounties can be employed to mitigate smart contract risks. Over time, common errors in smart contracts written in popular languages such as Ethereum's Solidity become more familiar, and high-quality teams know to look for common attack vectors.

Miner risk deals with the possibility that transaction processing entities behave maliciously towards certain transactions. This depends on the correct ordering and execution of transactions sent to a DeFi smart contract. It operates at an analogous level to settlement risk in centralized finance, involving the finalization of transactions, although the nature of the threat is different. In blockchain systems, users typically send a transaction to the network along with a fee to the miner that successfully processes it into a block

Miners take proposed transactions and decide the order in which to execute them. However, a miner need not execute transactions in fee order. A miner can choose to execute a lower-fee transaction ahead of a higher-fee transaction, if that transaction is particularly valuable to them, or in return for a side payment from the originator of the lower-fee transaction. Such behavior allows for a form of market manipulation like front-running in high-frequency trading. By manipulating the order of execution, a miner can effectively allow certain parties to compound returns faster than others. Some view "miner extractable value" as inevitable in any system based on public block chains, which is legitimate if structured transparently and fairly. This is a topic of active debate in the DeFi community

Oracle risk involves the potential that data external to the blockchain on which a DeFi contract relies is inaccurate or has been manipulated. Oracle-dependent DeFi protocols are susceptible to attacks in which oracle providers can manipulate the price observed on-chain. If on-chain asset holders can do this, they can increase the value of their on-chain asset or decrease the value of other participants' assets. Re-marking below a liquidation threshold could lead to assets being sold to the highest or first bidder. If an oracle uses a centralized data source, such as a feed from CoinMarketCap for prices, this represents a source of centralized trust and vulnerability. An oracle can be decentralized by using multiple data sources or by incentivizing providers to submit data. Decentralization makes it difficult for a small number of participants to manipulate prices. On the other hand, payments to data providers must be designed effectively for fairness and incentive compatibility to ensure accurate information. Poor mechanism design may make it profitable to manipulate oracle data feeds. There have already been several successful DeFi oracle attacks.

Operational

Even though DeFi activity is highly automated, human operators still play a crucial role. The more decentralized a service, the less risk there is associated with any single point of failure. Auxiliary services may be centralized even when the DeFi service is highly decentralized. At the same time, greater decentralization can make it harder to respond effectively when something goes wrong. The fewer people who have unique power to break a service, the fewer who have the power to fix it.

Routine maintenance and upgrades may be more difficult to implement for decentralized services, or may create vulnerabilities, especially given the composability of DeFi. This would also include ongoing network and node connectivity and considerations related to security and cyber risks. Code forks are options for groups seeking to alter elements of DeFi services, providing an "exit" option for minorities that prefer a different set of parameters. In some cases, a fork may become more popular than the original service. When there is already significant activity on a platform, however, forks can be costly and confusing for participants. They can also be employed for malicious purposes, including to mislead users.

Key management is a potential problem for all blockchain-based systems. Platforms identify users and their assets through cryptographic key pairs. Because DeFi services are non-custodial, they place the key management burden on their users in return for removing dependencies on centralized service providers. A variety of techniques including requiring multiple signatures (multi-sig), social recovery and custody arrangements have been developed to address key management risks for digital assets. Governance mechanisms for DeFi and other blockchain-based services raise complex potential risks. "One-token, one-vote" may be exploited when participation rates are low, token control is concentrated, or participants can bribe each other to vote in their favor. Centralized exchanges may take advantage of the voting power of tokens in their custody to exert undue influence in governance. Specialized DeFi market participants may engage in activities analogous to activist investing, deliberately acquiring significant shares of governance tokens for a service. With enough voting power, these investors could change the parameters, allowing them to drain liquidity pools.

Even though many of the mechanisms incorporated into DeFi governance systems have a history in academic literature, their behavior with large numbers of participants and millions or billions of dollars at stake remains unproven. Moreover, a recent research paper presents evidence that DeFi token holdings are heavily concentrated, in ways that are not entirely transparent

Redress of disputes is a final category of governance risks. Once a smart contract has executed, the output cannot be modified or reversed just because an individual actor, or a governmental authority, orders it to be. When participants believe they are entitled to redress for some failure of the system or malicious act, arbitration may be incorporated into the DeFi service through multi-sig arrangements or be decentralized through a prediction market or crowdsourcing mechanism. However, these novel mechanisms have their own limitations, for instance, compared to judicial or administrative orders. With a well-designed DeFi service, operational risks may be measured in real time and actively mitigated. DeFi transaction ledgers are public, so malicious activities may be tracked more easily than in analogous cases for centralized finance.

Legal compliance

DeFi can be used to get around legal or regulatory requirements. The activities could take place with any service that uses digital assets. Money laundering, for example, is an issue for both traditional centralised cryptocurrency exchanges and DeFi DEXs. We only present a brief description of risks in this area because the focus of this research is on the unique difficulties and potential of DeFi.

While a DeFi structure may not enhance the possibility of such infractions per se, it may make enforcement more difficult. DeFi services' decentralised, non-custodial, and composable structure, for example, may make it impossible to identify a responsible party.

Regulatory regimes centered on intermediaries as regulated processors of transaction information may not be compatible with a disintermediated market structure.

Financial crime is the violation of anti-money laundering/counter-terrorism financing (AML/ CFT) rules, financial sanctions, and related regulatory frameworks. Because users are pseudonymous by default, transactions are resistant to blockage, assets are resistant to seizure, and many transactions involve non-custodial wallets not directly tied to individuals, DeFi transactions involving natively digital assets may be difficult to regulate through traditional AML/CFT controls. Despite the fact that DeFi transactions are generally public and traceable, future privacy-enhancing protocols and/or tools may pose further regulatory issues. Several approaches have been developed to comply with the Financial Action Task Force's (FATF) 2019 anti-money laundering guidance for digital asset service providers, but more work remains and could be impacted by new guidance proposed in March 2021 that could require know-your-customer (KYC) compliance from DeFi services. The use of non-custodial solutions and self-hosted wallets in DeFi, in particular, presents a challenge to the requirement that identifying metadata be collected and sent for every transaction link.

Fraud and market manipulation are premeditated deceptions, misappropriations, and other attempts to take advantage of investors. Rather than third-party attacks, we refer to activities carried out or enabled by DeFi developers.

For example, "rug pulls" or exit scams entail getting consumers to deposit funds into a seemingly legitimate DeFi service, only to have the cash drained by the developers, who then vanish. Regulatory evasion refers to the failure to meet regulatory responsibilities by performing comparable duties in a different technical method. It may entail purposefully obscuring activity or concealing the jurisdictional characteristics of transactions. However, the fact that a fresh activity resembles an established one does not inherently entail regulatory arbitrage. Poorly drafted regulatory responsibilities may be seen as a risk factor for DeFi. All of the major types of DeFi activity can be considered as alternatives to regulated financial services. It is beyond the scope of this research to say whether they are subject to similar categories, and the responses will differ by jurisdiction.

Emergent risks

Emergent risks are caused by the interaction effects of several events, resulting in failure instances that are not represented in an independent risk assessment of each service. Classic recent instances include "too big to fail" banks and scenarios in which nominally unrelated events, such as individual mortgage foreclosures, become strongly interconnected and cause cascading consequences via securitization chains. Other instances include systemwide liquidity collapse owing to bank runs or markets "freezing up," which occurs when parties are unwilling to deal due to perceived risk.

Dynamic interactions among a potentially infinite number of interconnected DeFi components may result in risks not present in any one service. Furthermore, because DeFi operates in a worldwide market, operations are not limited to specific countries or business segments, as they are when transactions are conducted in a national sovereign currency. Unless authorities can successfully curb cross-border DeFi activity, firebreaks to systemic default contagion may be less effective than in traditional finance. As DeFi services begin to interact with traditional financial systems, interaction risks will increase.

In exceptionally volatile or turbulent market conditions, flash crashes or price cascades may occur, exacerbated by leverage in the DeFi system.

Unlike traditional markets, where primary dealers and brokers can manually intervene when many defaults occur at the same time, the permissionless, algorithmic nature of DeFi may make it impossible to halt cascades. DeFi services that automatically liquidate collateral enable liquidators to compete for the purchase of that collateral, often offering a fixed discount as an incentive. However, when there is a flash crash or extreme market volatility, there may be so many liquidations and the drop in the price of the collateral may be so precipitous that liquidators or others will experience huge losses. It is difficult to assess such danger. Most classic financial models assume that liquidations are always successful because a trusted third party (exchange, broker, or dealer) will liquidate a position when it is no longer profitable. This is only true in DeFi when liquidators can execute a profitable liquidation. If cascades continue for an extended period of time, liquidators stop liquidating and traditional value-at-risk (VaR) models fail.

This failure is reminiscent of the 2008 financial crisis, when centralised third parties that enforced liquidations, such as AIG, failed.

This type of risk can be estimated using tools like agent-based simulation, which models rational behavior for all principal parties (borrowers, lenders, traders, and liquidators) and then runs millions of event-based Monte Carlo simulations – models for predicting outcomes in situations with random variables – to estimate worst-case loss. These simulations, unlike standard financial Monte Carlo simulations, investigate scenarios in which financial assumptions such as no-arbitrage and quick liquidation are invalid. Corrections to standard value-at-risk (VAR) models can be determined using such models, resulting in estimates of default probability as a function of characteristics such as volatility.

Policy approaches

This section discusses the primary areas where DeFi may intersect with policy and legislation. It is important to note that it lays out essential concerns and possibilities but does not provide prescriptive answers because jurisdictions differ in their aims, regulatory systems, and market makeup. The approaches discussed here are intended to be sufficiently broad to be applicable in a wide range of situations. The rest of this section contains tools and resources.

Trust-minimized execution, non-custodial services, and composable architectures may put present regulations at jeopardy. As discussed earlier, DeFi can introduce new risks while also helping to alleviate established problems in financial services. Many of the fundamental concerns for policymakers – how decentralisation makes it difficult to identify regulatory topics, increased dangers due to automation, and how borderless software code hampers the application of territorial rules – are extensions of issues that affect all digital assets. Others, like as the construction of building blocks with various potential use cases and integrations, or the tokenized governance incentive systems, are less well-known. Given the interdisciplinary character of DeFi, an integrated strategy and vision are required.

In general, it may be prudent to pursue a technologically neutral approach to balancing regulatory regime aims with supporting innovation and market development. Policymakers, like any other regulatory activity, should strive for DeFi laws that are fair, efficient, effective, and enforceable.

The first step is to identify the relevant objectives and associated categories of policy and regulation. Common goals for financial regulation include protection of investors and other consumers; market efficiency and integrity; capital formation; financial inclusion; prevention of illicit activity; safety and soundness; and financial stability. Each provides a distinctive logic for certain kinds of rules. For example, regulators focused on investor protection are typically concerned that custodians are not able to abscond with funds. The noncustodial nature of DeFi may alleviate some of these worries, while creating new ones (as outlined in Section 2).

DeFi activity spans many domains of financial regulation, including securities, derivatives, exchanges, investment management, bank supervision, financial crime, consumer finance, insurance, risk management and macroprudential oversight. A coherent overarching strategy is important and could be delegated to a cross entity taskforce or similar body. Some DeFi activity patterns will clearly match established legal categories; others will not. A range of policy actions may be adopted for DeFi, including:

A range of policy actions may be adopted for DeFi, including:

- Forbearance: decision that no new regulations are needed
- Warnings: issuance of warning to users/ consumers

- Enforcement: determinations that existing rules already cover the relevant actors and activities and have not been complied with
- Opt-in: provide the option to become subject to regulations in return for certain protections, even though there is no legal requirement
- Pruning regulations: eliminate regulatory requirements that are no longer essential in a DeFi context
- Limited license frameworks: the possibility of obtaining licenses of limited scope or under size thresholds, with light-touch requirements
- Prohibitive measures: prohibit certain activities in the DeFi sector
- New license types: address risks with new categories designed for DeFi
- Issuing guidance or expectations: craft new frameworks, often with a public comment or consultation included before its official release

An effective regulatory response to DeFi will very certainly entail a mix of existing regulation, retrofitted regulation, and new, tailored regulation.

The European Union's comprehensive Markets in Crypto Assets (MiCA) proposal is part of a developing body of digital asset-specific law. However, most governments have yet to implement customized frameworks.

Most financial regulatory regimes focus on those "doing business" in a specific regulated activity, such as "selling," "arranging," or "running" some scheme or exchange, or "making" an offer (or similar).

Historically, the appropriate government agency has been fairly clear and focused on who ultimately controls an activity. Similarly, there are also exclusions for service providers who only supply infrastructure, data, or other tools that allow others to layer on their financial services. Frameworks consider definable and centralised operators who provide certain financial end goods and services but are not always the underlying builders.

However, in the DeFi setting, there may not be a central body doing the required functions. The software engineers and token holders may be easily identified, but individuals in roles that are typical regulatory touchpoints are not. Because the protocols are decentralised, even when operators are recognised, they may lack the capacity to modify DeFi services or stop transactions. Smart contracts have the ability to interact with assets held by other smart contracts that are not directly tied with a specific user. Regulators will need to determine who is accountable and when a center of responsibility must be established. It may be able to accomplish this through careful examination of services, even if they are supposedly decentralised.

Legal systems frequently incorporate methods for vicarious secondary "controlling person," "responsible officer," or aiding-and-abetting responsibility based on requirements such as knowledge or foresight of potentially detrimental outcomes. If developers of a DeFi service or others involved with the DeFi business might have detected and addressed legal compliance issues, policymakers must examine whether mandating that they do so is acceptable.

Regulating the creation of software, on the other hand, presents significant questions about free speech and administrability that should be carefully studied. The transnational nature of blockchain networks and digital assets additionally complicates DeFi regulation at the national or subnational level.

Available policy tools

While not identical, policy approaches may be influenced by how digital assets were initially addressed. During the 2017 ICO boom, few authorities had structures or expertise appropriate for purpose, while considerable funds flowed into new platforms that claimed to be outside the regulatory perimeter, seemingly out of nowhere.

Some of the early comments may be relevant in the context of DeFi.

Units of specialised regulation. A focused desk with competent people can serve as an initial entry point for gaining experience in new technology, interacting with the industry, and providing guidance. This intelligence can be shared with policymakers, and steps such as issuing non-action letters under existing regulatory frameworks could be taken. These organization s may help DeFi projects gain legal clarity and support early-stage engagement with authorities. Regulators should also invest in technology and technical skills to better comprehend these markets. This strategy has been employed by several jurisdictions. The US Securities and Exchange Commission (SEC), for example, established the FinHub section (which will be upgraded to a permanent stand-alone office in late 2020), while Switzerland's financial regulator, FINMA, established the FinTech Desk. Despite its tiny size and limited authority at first, they quickly became a vital point of contact for both internal and external populations.

Incentives for information flow. One of the most prevalent techniques of financial regulation is disclosure. Even if the relevance of existing disclosure rules on DeFi platforms is questionable, efforts to encourage comprehensive and uniform information sharing may be beneficial for regulatory analysis. The Monetary Authority of Singapore spent a substantial chunk of its ICO regulation on white paper evaluations.

Regulatory sandboxes. Policymakers may elect to create regulatory forbearance programmes, such as sandboxes, in which enterprises can test and operate their technologies in a limited scope, and so with limited regulatory risks.

The scope of such regulatory "carve-outs" can be defined by activities, financial thresholds, territorial or customer limits, and combined with reporting obligations to ensure that the regulatory authority gains experience in new technology, interacts with the industry, and responds if new risks emerge. However, a regulatory authority's lack of clarity regarding the trajectory may inadvertently inhibit innovation, and there may be commercial risks for businesses working in sandboxes without specified safe harbours.

The sandbox allows start-ups to solve regulatory compliance problems while also providing regulators with a greater knowledge of the risks and rewards of a new space. A DeFi sandbox may go beyond previous models by establishing a mechanism of tracking the trajectory for projects trying to decentralise power over time in order to address some concerns while avoiding the creation of new ones. The UK Financial Conduct Authority (FCA) established a fintech sandbox regime that included a significant number of blockchain and digital asset services. It has, however, had limited impact for DeFi because Stablecoins are believed to be outside the scope of the FCA. Others, such as Colombia's "la Arenera" sandbox, have used a similar strategy. DeFi sandboxes will need to be carefully structured to avoid prematurely signaling regulatory clearance.

A regulation-free zone, as developed in Busan, South Korea, is a variation on this strategy. Specific jurisdictions within a country may allow enterprises to operate under a limited set of regulations (typically not totally "regulation-free") in order to allow for service innovation and testing under this paradigm.

Clearing up simple instances. There will always be some new activities that obviously raise regulatory red flags, others that do not, and some that fall somewhere in the middle. Policymakers and regulators can sometimes restrict the zone of uncertainty and incentivise compliance efforts by taking on the easier situations first, especially those where intervention is not necessary.

A safe harbor policy, which explicitly excludes from regulation services that match specific criteria, is a more formal way for identifying easy cases. The 2017 investigative report on the DAO was the US SEC's first public declaration in the ICO case.44 It stated that while bitcoin is not regarded a security, a token developed for investment purposes is.

Furthermore, because the DAO had already been shut down, no enforcement action was required. Despite leaving many points unaddressed, the report highlighted the SEC's approach and concerns, allowing for future discussion.

Bringing government action together. In some circumstances, bringing together multiple government organization s for a coordinated response may be beneficial. In the United States, five federal regulatory agencies (the SEC, the Commodity Futures Trading Commission [CFTC], the Federal Deposit Insurance Corporation [FDIC], the Office of the Comptroller of the Currency [OCC], and the Federal Reserve Board) modified the "Volcker Rule."

This list is not meant to be exhaustive. It also does not presume the policymakers' eventual course of action. These strategies are equally applicable if DeFi services are eventually discovered to be covered by existing requirements, outside the regulatory perimeter, or subject to new, customized laws.

BLOCKCHAIN TECHNOLOGIES ON THE INDUSTRY

Banks, governments, and other financial institutions were among the first to use blockchain technology, and they continue to be among the fastest growing blockchain users. The sophisticated tools being developed to manage and move money will transform our world in unanticipated ways, so it's only natural that financial technology (fintech) will come on board. Banking was the first industry to identify Bitcoin's threat and, later, the potential of blockchain to alter the industry. The banking industry is highly regulated, and the fees for establishing and operating a bank are considerable. These stringent restrictions have served as both an insulator and a barrier for the entire sector, as well as a burden. The use of rapid, efficient, digital money that does not incur the cost of handling cash and is traceable as it flows through the financial system was both enticing and perilous.

The notion that value can exist outside of the supervision of central authorities attracted the curiosity of financial organizations and governments that sponsor currencies.

Initially, financial organizations and governments attempted to stifle blockchain through regulation. Today, they are embracing blockchain by investing in it across the board. The Securities and Exchange Commission (SEC) of the United States issued a warning to investors in 2013 and 2014 regarding the possible risks of virtual currency investments. The concern was that investors would be tempted by the promise of huge returns and not be wary enough of the new and cutting-edge investment field. The SEC ranked digital currency as one of the top 10 hazards to investors. As bitcoin develops traction across industries, the SEC is ready to interact with corporations and investors.

Not even two years later, nations all over the world, including the United Kingdom, Canada, Australia, and China, began looking into how they could develop their own digital currencies, taking cryptocurrencies for themselves and putting money on the blockchain. The tipping point came when they realised that the advantages began to exceed the hazards.

For several years, Bitcoin had been able to withstand hacking attempts, even when many government systems were compromised, making it an enticing method to try.

Blockchain technological advancements claimed to be able to manage the billions of transactions required to maintain economies, making a cryptocurrency practical at scale. Blockchains are permanent and unchangeable records of every transaction. Putting a country's money supply on a blockchain controlled by a central bank would be completely transformational since there would be a permanent record of every financial transaction, existing at some level inside their blockchain record, even if it wasn't available by the public.

Blockchain technology and digital currencies would reduce risk and fraud while providing them with complete control over monetary policy and taxation. It would not be anonymous in the same way that Bitcoin was at first. In reality, it would provide them with a complete and auditable trace of every digital transaction undertaken by individuals and businesses. It may even empower central banks to take over the job of commercial banks in money circulation. The prospect of what the future of banking will look like can be both frightening and exhilarating. Consumers may now pay friends nearly quickly using their phones in almost any sort of currency or cryptocurrency. More and more retail businesses are accepting cryptocurrencies as payment for goods and accepting payment from customers. Using Bitcoin is more common than not in Kenya. However, for the vast majority of the population, this is still not a viable alternative. Western markets are still in the early stages of acceptance.

Given that the majority of people's money is trapped into legal tender issued by governments or assets within existing government systems, fintech technologies must integrate with these existing systems before blockchain or digital currencies become widely used. If regulators can figure out how to tax and register accounts, mainstream adoption of customer-facing wallets with digitised tokens will be two or three years away. Blockchain will be used much more quickly in the business-to-business industry.

A production-hardened system, with the accompanying policies and operations, will be available in less than two years. Ripple and R3, among others, have worked tirelessly to make this a reality. These systems will initially focus on the institutional construction of electronic deposit representations.

These are letters of credit between internal organizational departments and trusted partners such as vendors. Regulators, central banks, and monetary authorities are all substantially investing to make this a reality. Canada and Singapore have been moving at breakneck speed.

Know your customer (KYC) and anti-money laundering (AML) requirements require banks to know who they do business with and to ensure that they are not involved in money laundering or terrorism. Banks issuing cryptocurrency must first overcome substantial difficulties. In order to comply with KYC and AML rules, they must know the identities of every persons who use their currency. People's bank accounts, with the exception of centralised, are already debit and credit service of transactions, similar to distributed ledgers in blockchains. The first candidates in this field will be regions where regulators, banks, and central banks collaborate. Singapore and Dubai are two obvious options because they already have blockchain programs in place.

It is difficult to estimate the transaction volume required for a blockchain to handle the currency of an economy such as the United Kingdom or the United States. The United States alone processes billions of transactions per day and more than $17 trillion in value per year. That's a lot of pressure for a new technology! If the country's monetary supply was jeopardised, it would be paralysed. The International Monetary Fund, World Bank, Bank for International Settlements, and central bankers from around the world have gathered to study blockchain technology. Adopting a blockchain as the technology to support bank transfers and interbank settlement would be the first step toward faster and cheaper money. Official digital currencies for everyday use by regular folks would arrive much later.

Individual customers would not see a direct cost savings from using a blockchain for interbank settlement. The savings would be shown in the bank's bottom line as cost reductions for intermediary fees.

For the foreseeable future, consumers will require retail stores and commercial banks. However, millennials have already embraced app-based payments such as PayPal, Venmo, Cash, and others. They are unconcerned about a new method of payment via their phones. The major challenge is that if all money is digital, any compromise may be disastrous.

It is possible that the architecture of blockchain systems will be sufficient. The problem could alternatively be that the code within the system gets run in an unexpected manner, as happened in the Ethereum decentralised autonomous organization (DAO) breach. If the cryptocurrency ran on a typical public blockchain, then 51 percent of the network's nodes would have to agree to repair the problem.

Putting an agreement in place could take a long time, which would be inconvenient for enterprises and individuals who require solid and safe money at all times.

Blockchain was originally only a computer science word describing how to structure and share data. Blockchains are now regarded as the "fifth evolution" of computing. Blockchains are an innovative way to distributed databases. The innovation stems from repurposing old technologies in novel ways. They can be thought of as distributed databases that are controlled by a group of people and are used to store and share information. There are numerous kinds of blockchains and applications.

Blockchain is a multifaceted technology that is being integrated across platforms and hardware all over the world. A blockchain is a data structure that enables the creation of a digital ledger of data and its distribution among a network of independent participants.

There are numerous sorts of blockchains. Public blockchains, such as Bitcoin, are large, distributed networks that are run through a native token. They're open for anyone to participate at any level and have open-source code that their community maintains. Permissioned blockchains, such as Ripple, control roles that individuals can play within the network. They're still large and distributed systems that use a native token. Their core code may or may not be open source. Private blockchains tend to be smaller and do not utilize a token. Their membership is closely controlled.

These types of blockchains are favored by consortiums that have trusted members and trade confidential information.

All three types of blockchains use cryptography to enable each network participant to administer the ledger in a secure manner without the need for a centralised authority to enforce the rules.

One of the most essential and powerful elements of blockchains is the absence of central authority from database structures. Blockchains generate permanent transaction records and histories, but nothing is truly permanent. The record's longevity is determined by the network's longevity. In the context of blockchains, this means that a huge section of a blockchain community must agree to modify the information and is encouraged not to change the data.

It is extremely impossible to delete or remove data that has been recorded in a blockchain. When someone wishes to add a record to a blockchain, commonly known as a transaction or an entry, individuals with validation control in the network verify the proposed transaction. This is where things get complicated because each blockchain has its own take on how this should function and who can validate a transaction.

A blockchain is a peer-to-peer system that manages data flow without the use of a central authority. A broad distributed network of independent users is one of the most important strategies to remove central control while ensuring data integrity. This means that the machines that comprise the network are spread across multiple locations. These machines are frequently referred to as full nodes. Blockchains are not just decentralised, but they frequently use a cryptocurrency to prevent network corruption. A cryptocurrency is a digital token with monetary value. Cryptocurrencies, like equities, are exchanged on exchanges.

Each blockchain's cryptocurrency works a little differently. Essentially, the software pays the hardware to run. The blockchain protocol is the software. Bitcoin, Ethereum, Ripple, Hyperledger, and Factom are examples of well-known blockchain protocols. The hardware comprises of the entire nodes that secure the network's data.

Blockchains are widely considered as the "fifth evolution" of computing, the Internet's missing trust layer. This is one of the reasons why so many people are interested in this subject.

Blockchains have the potential to increase confidence in digital data. It is nearly impossible to erase or edit information after it has been entered into a blockchain database. This capability has never before existed.

When data is permanent and dependable in digital form, it allows you to do business online in ways that were previously only conceivable offline.

Everything that was previously analogue, such as property rights and identity, can now be established and preserved online. Slow commercial and banking activities, such as money transfers and fund settlements, can now be completed very instantly. The ramifications of secure digital records for the global economy are tremendous.

The first apps were established to capitalize on the safe digital value transfer enabled by blockchains through the trading of their native currencies. These included the movement of money and assets, among other things. However, the blockchain networks' capabilities extend far beyond the transfer of currency.

The author of the 2008 whitepaper that first presented Bitcoin is an unidentified programmer or cohort who goes under the name Satoshi Nakamoto. Until 2010, Nakamoto worked on Bitcoin with a number of other open-source developers. This individual or group has since withdrawn from the project and handed over management to renowned Bitcoin core developers. There have been numerous claims and ideas about Nakamoto's identity, but none of them have been confirmed as of this writing.

What Nakamoto did invent, however, is an incredible peer-to-peer payment system that allows users to send Bitcoin, the value transfer token, directly and without the need for an intermediary to hold the two parties accountable. The network itself works as an intermediary, confirming transactions and ensuring that no one attempts to game the system by spending Bitcoins twice.

Nakamoto's goal was to fill a significant gap in digital trust, and the blockchain concept was his solution. It answers the ultimate human difficulty, the Byzantine general's problem, especially online: How can you trust the information you're given and the individuals who offer it to you when self-interest, hostile third parties, and other such things might fool you? Many Bitcoin supporters believe that blockchain technology will be the missing piece that will allow societies to operate entirely online because it reframes trust by recording relevant information in a public space that cannot be removed and can always be referenced, making deception more difficult.

Blockchains combine several ancient technology that mankind has used for thousands of years in novel ways. Cryptography and payment, for example, are combined to form cryptocurrency. Cryptography is the art of communicating securely in the presence of third parties. Payment via a token that symbolises values is something humans have done for a long time, but when combined, it generates cryptocurrencies and something altogether new. Cryptocurrency allows you to take the concept of money and bring it online, allowing you to trade value securely via a token.

Blockchains also use hashing (the process of converting large amounts of data into short, fixed-length values). Hashing also incorporates an old method known as Merkle trees, which take several hashes and compress them into a single hash while still proving each piece of data that was independently. Finally, blockchains are ledgers, which have been used by civilization for thousands of years to keep financial records. When all of these old models are combined and made available online through a distributed database, they become revolutionary.

Bitcoin was created largely for the purpose of sending the Bitcoin cryptocurrency. However, the inventors rapidly discovered that it had far greater potential. With this in mind, they designed the Bitcoin blockchain to be capable of recording more than just token movement data. The Bitcoin blockchain is the world's oldest and one of the largest blockchains.

It is made up of thousands of nodes that operate the Bitcoin protocol. The protocol is responsible for establishing and safeguarding the blockchain.

In a nutshell, the blockchain is a public database of all Bitcoin network transactions, and nodes are computers that record inputs into that ledger. The rules that govern this system are defined by the Bitcoin protocol.

Nodes protect the network by mining Bitcoin, a cryptocurrency. As an incentive for processing transactions and documenting them in the blockchain, new Bitcoins are created. Nodes are also compensated for confirming transactions.

Anyone with a computer may run the Bitcoin protocol and mine the token. It's an open-source initiative that grows in popularity as more people join the network.

The fewer participants there are, the more centralised the system becomes – and centralization weakens the system. The enormous number of independent nodes that are globally spread is the fundamental factor that makes Bitcoin a secure system.

Successful miners have resilient systems that outperform slower miners. Earlier in its history, you could run the Bitcoin protocol on a desktop computer and earn Bitcoins. To have any chance of ever obtaining Bitcoins, you must must invest in costly specialised equipment or use a cloud service.

To create a message in the Bitcoin blockchain, you must first transfer some Bitcoin from one account to another. When you send a Bitcoin transaction, the message is broadcast to the whole network. Because the message is stored in the Bitcoin blockchain, it is difficult to change it after it has been transmitted. Because of this feature, it is critical that you always choose your message carefully and never broadcast sensitive information.

Broadcasting the identical message to thousands of nodes and then storing it in the token's ledger forever can quickly add up. As a result, Bitcoin necessitates that you keep your communications brief. The current character limit is only 40.

THE STRUCTURE OF BLOCKCHAINS

Blockchains are composed of three core parts:

Block: A list of transactions recorded into a ledger over a given period. The size, period, and triggering event for blocks is different for every blockchain. Not all blockchains are recording and securing a record of the movement of their cryptocurrency as their primary objective. But all blockchain do record the movement of their cryptocurrency or token. Think of the transaction as simply being the recording of data. Assigning a value to it (such as happens in a financial transaction) is used to interpret what that data means.

Chain: A hash that links one block to another, mathematically "chaining" them together. This is one of the most difficult concepts in blockchain to comprehend. It's also the magic that glues blockchains together and allows them to create mathematical trust. The hash in blockchain is created from the data that was in the previous block. The hash is a fingerprint of this data and locks blocks in order and time. Although blockchains are a relatively new innovation, hashing is not.

Hashing was invented over 30 years ago. This old innovation is being used because it creates a one-way function that cannot be decrypted. A hashing function creates a mathematical algorithm that maps data of any size to a bit string of a fixed size. A bit string is usually 32 characters long, which then represents the data that was hashed. The Secure Hash Algorithm (SHA) is one of some cryptographic hash functions used in blockchains. SHA-256 is a common algorithm that generates an almost-unique, fixedsize 256-bit (32-byte) hash. For practical purposes, think of a hash as a digital fingerprint of data that is used to lock it in place within the blockchain.

Network: The network is composed of "full nodes." Think of them as the computer running an algorithm that is securing the network. Each node contains a complete record of all the transactions that were ever recorded in that blockchain. The nodes are located all over the world and can be operated by anyone. It's difficult, expensive, and time-consuming to operate a full node, so people don't do it for free. They're incentivized to operate a node because they want to earn cryptocurrency.

The underlying blockchain algorithm rewards them for their service. The reward is usually a token or cryptocurrency, like Bitcoin.

The terms Bitcoin and blockchain are often used interchangeably, but they're not the same. Bitcoin has a blockchain. The Bitcoin blockchain is the underlying protocol that enables the secure transfer of Bitcoin. The term Bitcoin is the name of the cryptocurrency that powers the Bitcoin network. The blockchain is a class of software, and Bitcoin is a specific cryptocurrency.

Blockchain Applications

Blockchain applications are founded on the premise that the network acts as an arbitrator. This type of system is a harsh and unforgiving environment.

Computer code is made into law, and laws are carried out exactly as they were written and interpreted by the network. Computers lack the same social biases and behaviors that humans do.

The network is unable to decipher intent (at least not yet). Insurance contracts arbitrated on a blockchain have been extensively researched as a use case based on this concept. Another intriguing feature that blockchains provide is flawless record keeping. They can be used to build a detailed timeline of who did what when. Many industries and regulatory organizations devote endless hours to assessing this issue. Blockchain-enabled record keeping will alleviate some of the constraints that come with attempting to interpret the past. The invention of blockchains began with the creation of Bitcoin. It demonstrated that a group of people who had never met before could operate online within a system that was desensitised to cheating others on the network.

The first Bitcoin network was created to protect the Bitcoin cryptocurrency. It has over 5,000 complete nodes and is scattered internationally. It's primarily used to trade Bitcoin and exchange value, but the community realised the network's potential for much more. It is also being used to secure other smaller blockchains and blockchain applications because to its size and time-tested security. The Ethereum network is the second stage of the blockchain concept's progression.

It uses the traditional blockchain topology and adds an internal programming language. It, like Bitcoin, has over 5,000 complete nodes and is distributed internationally. Ethereum is largely used for trading Ether, creating smart contracts, and establishing decentralised autonomous organization s (DAOs). It's also used to protect blockchain apps and smaller blockchains.

The Factom network represents the third stage of blockchain evolution. It employs a lighter consensus mechanism, involves voting, and retains far more data. It was designed primarily to protect data and the system. Factom employs federated nodes and an infinite number of auditing nodes.

Because its network is limited, it attaches itself into other distributed networks by constructing bridges across the carries blockchains. Blockchains are effective tools because they enable honest systems to self-correct without the need for a third party to enforce the rules. They achieve rule enforcement through their consensus algorithm.

Consensus is the process of reaching an agreement among a group of typically distrusting shareholders in the blockchain world. These are the network's complete nodes. The full nodes validate transactions that are submitted into the network in order for them to be recorded as part of the ledger. Each blockchain has its own algorithms for reaching consensus on new entries inside its network. Because each blockchain generates different types of data, there are numerous models for achieving consensus. Some blockchains trade value, while others store data and secure systems and contracts.

Bitcoin, for example, exchanges the value of its currency among network participants. Because the tokens have a market value, the requirements for performance, scalability, consistency, threat model, and failure model will be more stringent. Bitcoin functions under the assumption that a malevolent attacker may want to tamper with the trade history in order to steal tokens. Bitcoin prevents this by employing a consensus model known as "proof of work," which answers the Byzantine general's problem: "How do you know that the information you're looking at hasn't been modified internally or externally?" Because modifying or manipulating data is virtually always feasible, data reliability is a significant issue in computer science.

Most blockchains are built on the assumption that they will be attacked by outside forces or by system users. The sort of consensus algorithm used to settle their ledger will be determined by the predicted threat and the network's trust in the nodes that administer the blockchain.

Bitcoin and Ethereum, for example, anticipate a high level of threat and employ a powerful consensus method known as proof of work. The network is untrustworthy.

Blockchains intended to record financial transactions between known parties, on the other hand, can employ a lighter and speedier consensus. Their requirement for high-speed transactions is more pressing. Because of the comparably limited participants in the network and the necessity for rapid finality for each transaction, proof of work is too slow and costly for them to operate.

There are hundreds of blockchains and blockchain apps in use today. The entire world has been captivated with the concepts of moving money more quickly, incorporating and regulating in a distributed network, and developing secure applications and hardware. The majority of active blockchain applications focus on the movement of money or other kinds of value in a timely and cost-effective manner. Trading public business stock, paying employees in foreign nations, and swapping one currency for another are all examples of this.

Blockchains are also being employed as a component of software security stacks. The Department of Homeland Security (DHS) has been looking into blockchain software to safeguard Internet of Things (IoT) devices. Because it is especially sensitive to spoofing and other sorts of hacking, the

IoT world stands to benefit the most from this invention. IoT devices have also become increasingly prevalent, and their use in security has grown.

Examples include hospital systems, self-driving automobiles, and safety systems. Another intriguing blockchain invention is DAOs. This type of blockchain application is a novel method of organising and incorporating businesses online. DAOs have been used to organise and invest funds through the Ethereum blockchain.

Government-backed land record systems, identity, and international travel security applications are among the larger and longer-term blockchain initiatives now being investigated.

The potential of a blockchain-infused future have piqued the interest of entrepreneurs, governments, political parties, and humanitarians all around the world. Countries like the United Kingdom, Singapore, and the United Arab Emirates see it as a way to save money, establish new financial instruments, and retain clean records. They have active blockchain investments and efforts.

Blockchains have laid the groundwork for removing the requirement for trust from the equation. Whereas asking for "trust" used to be a significant matter, it's now a minor issue with blockchains. In addition, if trust is destroyed, the infrastructure that implements the rule might be lighter. Much of society is based on trust and the application of rules. Because blockchain will transform how we arrange value-based and socially based interactions, the social and economic ramifications of blockchain applications might be emotionally and politically controversial.

HISTORY OF ETHEREUM

Ethereum was first detailed in a whitepaper written in 2013 by Vitalik Buterin, a writer and programmer who was very involved in the Bitcoin ecosystem. Buterin sees far more promise in Bitcoin than the ability to shift value without the intervention of a central authority. He had been participating to the colored coin initiative within Bitcoin, which aimed to increase Bitcoin's utility beyond the sale of its native unit. Buterin thought that blockchain frameworks may be used to build additional corporate and government use cases that require a central authority to control them.

There was a heated controversy at the time about the Bitcoin network being "bloated" by a large number of low-value transactions from applications protecting themselves against Bitcoin. The main worry was that further apps based on the Bitcoin protocol would have difficulty scaling in volume. Bitcoin was not designed to handle the volume of transactions required by applications. Vitalik and many others observed that in order for people to build decentralised applications on the Bitcoin blockchain, either the blockchain needed a huge code upgrade or a new blockchain was needed entirely.

Bitcoin was already well-established at the time. The types of upgrades to core code that were required were clearly beyond what was realistically doable. Any improvements to the network would be stymied by Bitcoin's politics. In early 2014, Vitalik and his team founded the Ethereum Foundation to gather funds for the development of a blockchain with a built-in programming language.

During July and August of 2014, an online public crowd sale was used to support the initial development. The organization first raised a record $18 million by selling its cryptocurrency token, ether. People have been debating whether this type of crowd sale is lawful because it may be considered an unregulated security.

The project has not been hampered by the regulatory grey area. If anything, the project's cutting-edge character has drawn greater attention and talent to the foundation. Developers and businesspeople from all over the world who are dissatisfied and disillusioned have flocked to the project. Decentralization is viewed as the ideal answer to corrupt and tyrannical central governments.

The foundation was able to engage a big development team to build Ethereum thanks to the $18 million raised in the token sale. In July 2015, Ethereum Frontier, the initial version of the Ethereum network, was online to the public. It was a basic software version that only the most technically competent users could use to create their own apps.

The current Ethereum software release, Homestead, was released in 2016. It's a lot easier to use. Almost anyone can use the application template that is provided on it. It includes user interfaces that are intuitive and welcoming, as well as a strong and dedicated development community.

The next Ethereum release is called Metropolis. The primary distinction will be that applications will be completely created and thoroughly tested. It will also have more user-friendly applications and a broader market appeal, so that even nontechnical people will feel at ease using it.

Serenity is Ethereum's final planned phase of development. It is the point at which Ethereum will transition from a proof-of-work consensus mechanism (in which miners compete to build the next block) to a proof-of-stake approach. In a proof-of-stake model, nodes are picked pseudo-randomly, with their chances of being chosen growing as their stake in the network grows. Their stake is determined by the amount of cryptocurrency they own. The primary advantage of the modification will be a reduction in the cost of energy connected with proof of work. This may make it more appealing for individuals to run nodes in the network, increasing decentralisation and security.

Ethereum could be one of the most complicated blockchains ever created. It has its own Turing-complete programming language (a complete programming language that allows developers to create any form of application). The Ethereum protocol can accomplish almost anything that standard programming languages can do, only it's built inside a blockchain and so has the added benefits and security that comes with it. Ethereum can be used to build any software project you can think of.

Currently, the Ethereum ecosystem is the ideal environment to build decentralised applications. They provide excellent documentation and user-friendly interfaces that enable you to get up and running quickly. This system's primary features include rapid development time, security for small apps, and the ability for applications to readily connect with one another.

The Turing-complete programming language is the primary characteristic that distinguishes the Ethereum blockchain from the Bitcoin blockchain when it comes to developing new programs. Ethereum's scripting language allows for things like Twitter applications to be built in a few lines of code while remaining incredibly secure.

The Ethereum protocol has enabled the development of a completely new class of apps. You can use Ethereum to create a digital representation of almost any business, government, or organization's processes. At the moment, Ethereum's platform is being investigated for managing digital assets (a new class of asset that lives online and may represent a whole digital asset such as a Bitcoin token or a digital representation of a real-world asset such as corn commodities), financial instruments (such as mortgage-backed securities), recording ownership of assets such as land, and decentralised autonomous organization s (DAOs), a new way of organizing a business, nonprofit, government, or a corporation. DAOs are mostly constructed on the Ethereum platform.

Hacking a Blockchain

Ethereum has never been compromised. The hard fork in 2016 caused by the DAO attack noted in the "With tremendous power comes... great power" sidebar was not a system hack, but it is frequently characterized to as one. Ethereum performed flawlessly. The issue was that it was too flawless. When a big sum of money and the bulk of the system's users were threatened, it became imperative to restart the system.

On a blockchain like Ethereum, the only option to remedy an activity is to do a hard fork, which allows for a fundamental modification to the protocol. A hard fork invalidates previously valid blocks and transactions.

This was done by Ethereum to protect the monies that were being withdrawn from the first DAO by a user. Conceptually, the DAO hack was one of the largest bug bounties ever.

Having said that, numerous frauds and hacking attempts take place in the bitcoin arena. The majority of these attacks are aimed at centralised exchanges and applications. Many cybercriminals want to steal cryptocurrency. It has real value and is not protected by governments in the same way that ordinary money is. The anonymity of cryptocurrency also makes it appealing to criminals.

It is tough to apprehend and prosecute these criminals. However, the bitcoin community is fighting back and developing new security mechanisms. Hacking in a single location is far easier and less expensive than attempting to break into a decentralised network. When you hear about blockchain hacking, it's usually just a website or a bitcoin wallet that has been compromised, not the entire network. Ethereum smart contracts function similarly to contractual agreements, with the exception that there is no central party to enforce the contract. By applying economic pressure, the Ethereum protocol "enforces" smart contracts. They can also compel the implementation of a need if it exists within Ethereum, because Ethereum can show whether or not specific requirements were met. It is far more difficult to enforce if it does not exist within Ethereum.

Ethereum smart contracts are not yet legally enforceable and may never be because it is widely assumed that agreements may be enforced without the involvement of third parties. Governments have authority over legal systems. Governments, as they currently exist, are central authority – some with more or less consent and democratic norms. Each participant in an Ethereum smart contract has an unalienable vote. Artificial intelligence is not included in Ethereum smart contracts. This is an exciting potential for the near future. But, for the time being, Ethereum is simply software code that runs on a blockchain. Smart contracts on Ethereum are not secure. The DAO hack is a prime example of the problems that can arise. It's still early in the game, and pouring a lot of money into an unproven system isn't a good idea. Instead, try with little sums until all of the bugs in new contracts have been sorted out.

The Ethereum blockchain's coin is known as Ether. It was named after the material that was thought to pervade all space and allow the universe to exist. In this sense, Ether is the substance that enables Ethereum. Ether incentivizes the network to secure itself through proof-of-work mining in the same way that the Bitcoin token incentivizes the Bitcoin network. To run any programming on the Ethereum network, Ether is required. Ether is referred to as gas when used to execute a contract on Ethereum. The execution of code within a smart contract also costs some ether. This functionality enhances the token's utility. As long as people desire to use Ethereum for apps and contracts, ether will have a value that goes beyond speculation. Because of the explosive growth in the value of ether, it has become a popular token to speculate on. It is regularly traded on global marketplaces. Some new hedge funds are considering it as a potential investment vehicle. However, because to its volatility and lack of market depth, ether is a dangerous investment.

Blockchain helping in Insurance

Blockchain insurance technology is poised to transform how individuals and businesses purchase and acquire insurance coverage, and it is approaching faster than you might imagine! You must comprehend the ramifications of these new technologies that are just appearing on the horizon.

In this chapter, I explain how these new technologies work as well as their primary limitations. I demonstrate how Internet of Things (IoT) devices will work with insurance providers. I also discuss how self-executing blockchain contracts will influence policy and business structures.

This chapter prepares you for significant technological advances that may alter the burden of proof. You'll be able to make more informed judgments concerning blockchain-based insurance coverage and payments after reading this chapter. You'll learn how the cost of coverage affects you, as well as the various forms of coverage that will become available to you in the future. IoT devices, immutable data, decentralised autonomous organization s (DAOs), and smart contracts are all influencing the evolution of consumer insurance. The emergence of blockchains has enabled the confluence of all of these technologies.

Blockchains excel at a few tasks that will enable two fundamental transformations in how insurance is purchased and sold in the future: Individuals will be able to obtain more customized coverage, and new markets will open up that were previously unavailable owing to cost constraints.

Individual-centered insurance will allow for a dramatic shift in priorities. Asset management will be less important, allowing insurers to focus on risk assessment and matching supply and demand.

You could build a marketplace platform that protects clients. This new business could be organised in a variety of ways. One idea is an on-demand marketplace where consumers can post their requirements, which could be standardised by a custom smart contract or a Chain code contract.

You, as the insurer, might compute the premium for the specific demand using this type of model, based on historical data and other risk calculation criteria in your risk model. If the customer is pleased with the offer, he or she may bid or subscribe, depending on the demand model in use.

This new type of insurance could be offered by a peer-to-peer (P2P) or crowdfunded insurance company, as well as a traditional insurance company that incorporates the technology. In either case, both are created in a decentralised cryptocurrency ledger using smart contracts/Chain code to guarantee payment from the client to the investment in the event of a problem. Blockchain is important in this context since it permits a few things that were not practical or secure just a few years ago.

Because transaction fees are so minimal, blockchains enable near-frictionless value transfer, making micropayments possible. You can now enter new markets that did not previously have a functioning monetary or legal system, or in cases where the cost of transactions and disputes outweighed the advantage of providing coverage.

DAOs with smart contracts can be used to control big groups at a fraction of the cost and effort. This concept might be used to incorporate and manage your new firm, as well as possibly crowd-fund insurance platforms.

The self-executing feature of smart contracts may also shed light on many of the costs associated with claim adjustment and third-party processing and collection of cash.

The legality of all of this is still being debated. It is difficult to distinguish between privacy concerns and consumer rights. The country has its own set of rules and disclosures. When those regulations are met, however, the insurance sector and the consumer's experience with insurance will change dramatically. Microinsurance is insurance designed to protect low-income people from risks such as accidents, disease, and natural disasters. It is now more viable thanks to blockchain technology.

When considering microinsurance, keep two things in mind (which can go hand in hand):

- Insurance aimed at low-income households, farmers, and other businesses, with coverage tailored to individual needs – typically, a low-premium, index-based policy.
- Insurance that covers low-value goods or services.

The main problem with these types of contracts in typical insurance models is that their handling costs are disproportionately high, making it undesirable to serve these markets.

The ability of blockchains to transport value at extremely low cost, practically instantly anywhere in the globe, with no charge backs, offers up the possibility of serving more people at lower costs.

The main advantage of blockchain is that the establishment of smart contracts allows for secure transactions without the use of an intermediary, resulting in much lower insurance costs.

Blockchains allow for the establishment of new types of identities for both people and things. They are based on the traditional concept in which a certificate is issued by a certificate authority. A certificate for persons would be a document such as a birth certificate or a driver's license.

However, "items" have similar certificates that assist consumers in validating the quality and authenticity.

For years, these types of certificates have been counterfeited. More advanced security has been built into them, although this raises the expense.

Blockchains enable the storage of these traditional certificates in an unalterable history that anybody may access and reference. The ability to update such records when new events occur is a novel capability.

IoT devices can now automatically publish all kinds of data to their records and change their present status. Insurance will be only one of many businesses affected now that IoT devices can talk for themselves and have their histories and identities broadcast and sharable with third parties.

The Internet of Things (IoT) will most certainly have a substantial impact on three aspects of your life: the linked car, the connected house, and the connected self.

At its core, the Internet of Things (IoT) is a disruptive technology that will reshape a wide range of businesses, including automobile original equipment manufacturers (OEMs), home security, and cable and mobile providers. Insurance firms, particularly those dealing with property and casualty (P&C) coverage, are included in this mix.

The data collected by the sensors in the new appliances and devices, together with automation and increased control options, will open up new opportunities for new insurance businesses to emerge. When combined with blockchain decentralised ledgers and smart contracts, the entire process might be automated to levels previously unthinkable.

The new, always-on lifestyle that comes with such a profound shift in technology eliminates some current threats while introducing new ones, the most critical of which is information security. All of this implies that the risk factors must be reassessed. Self-driving cars, for example, will have a lower risk of accident because to the lack of human mistake, but the technology's reliability will be questioned until we have enough evidence from real-world application.

One of the most significant advantages that blockchain technology brings to the modern finance industry is the ability to conduct commercial transactions without the intervention of a third party, such as banks or intermediaries.

Simply said, a smart contract is a system that enables two parties to record their transaction in a blockchain. These contracts can be used for almost anything, ranging from the exchange of real things (with digital signatures) to the exchange of information or money.

The important security aspect here is that, unlike a traditional financial database, the information is spread among and checked by all computers in the network, resulting in a decentralised system. The data is unique and cannot be replicated; the audit trail is unchangeable. The centralised trust paradigm, in which middlemen such as bankers, brokers, and attorneys coordinate and certify the integrity of financial transactions and products exchanges, is at the heart of current business models.

Centralization introduces new security threats, such as data corruption and theft. Blockchains prevent this by establishing a decentralised system built on mutual distrust among all players, who keep each other in check.

To build such a system, you start with a distributed ledger that employs cryptocurrency (such as Bitcoin, Ethereum, or Factom), and each participant is both a user of the system and accountable for its upkeep and maintenance.

The goal, similar to conventional crowdfunding campaigns, is to pool resources from multiple businesses or individuals to cover an unanticipated shortfall in an insurance plan. For example, a retirement insurance plan may only kick in at the age of 65, but a person may be compelled to retire early due to unanticipated circumstances, necessitating the need for additional funds.

Economic disparities have expanded over time, and many people who are underinsured or uninsured could benefit from such a system.

DAOs are corporate entities that do not have full-time employees but can perform all of the functions of a standard corporation. The capacity to construct such an organization is directly related to the advancement of blockchain algorithms over the previous several years, which has resulted in what is widely referred to as blockchain 2.0.

A DAO is essentially a type of advanced smart contract. The DAO can be treated as a corporation in which all of its individual policy users are shareholders, but the corporation itself is never directly controlled by any particular group or individual.

Similarly, a DAO is never under the developers' authority, and they do not issue or refuse policies. It is solely a peer-to-peer insurance approach.

Although flaws in identity verification remain, this system will be rectified, and the same issues exist in present, centralised insurance systems.

Debunking Some Common Bitcoin Misconceptions

People are often suspicious of anything new, especially new things that aren't easy to understand. So, it's only natural that Bitcoin — a totally new currency unlike anything the world had ever seen before — would confound people, and a few misconceptions would result.

Here are some of the misconceptions you might have heard about Bitcoin:

Bitcoin was hacked. There has never been a successful attack on the Bitcoin blockchain that resulted in stolen Bitcoins. However, many central systems that use Bitcoin have been hacked. And wallets and Bitcoin exchanges are often hacked due to inadequate security. The Bitcoin community has fought back by developing elegant solutions to keep their coins safe, including wallet encryption, multiple signatures, offline wallets, paper wallets, and hardware wallets, just to name a few.

Bitcoin is used to extort people. Because of the semi-anonymous nature of Bitcoin, it's used in ransomware attacks. Hackers breach networks and hold them hostage until payment is made to them. Hospitals and schools have been victims of these types of attacks. However, unlike cash, which was favored by thieves in the past, Bitcoin always leaves a trail in the blockchain that investigators can follow.

Bitcoin is a pyramid scheme. Bitcoin is the opposite of a pyramid scheme from the point of view of Bitcoin miners. The Bitcoin protocol is designed like a cannibalistic arms race. Every additional miner prompts the protocol to increase the difficulty of mining. From a social point of view, Bitcoin is a pure market. The price of Bitcoins fluctuates based on market supply, demand, and perceived value. Bitcoin will collapse after 21 million coins are mined. Bitcoin has a limit to the number of tokens it will release. That number is hard-coded at 21 million. The estimated date of Bitcoin issuing its last coin is believed to be in the year 2140. No one can predict what will happen at that point, but miners will always earn some profit from transaction fees. Plus, users of the blockchain and the Bitcoins themselves will be incentivized to protect the network, because if mining stops, Bitcoins become vulnerable and so does the data that has been locked into the blockchain.

Enough computing power could take over the Bitcoin network. This is true, but it would be extremely difficult, with little to no reward. The more nodes that enter the Bitcoin network, the harder this type of attack becomes. In order to pull this off, an attacker would need the equivalent of all the energy production of Ireland. The payoff of this sort of attack is also extremely limited. It would only allow the attacker to roll back his own transaction. He couldn't take anybody else's Bitcoins or fake transactions or coins. Bitcoin is a good investment. Bitcoin is a new and interesting evolution in how people trade value. It isn't backed by any single government or organization, and it's only worth something because people are willing to trade it for goods and services. People's willingness and ability to utilize Bitcoin fluctuates a lot. It's an unstable investment that should be approached cautiously.

The new nature of financial transactions

Micropayments are the new transaction type. Credit card firms may employ blockchain technology to settle transactions, prevent fraud, and cut expenses.

Consumers in capitalistic cultures will always require global organization s such as Visa and MasterCard, which offer the benefit of delayed payment. Even if the backend changes, customers will still have the same access points. However, actual cards will be phased out. In reality, this is already happening, even without the use of blockchain technology. The consumer identities behind payments will be more resistant to theft as a result of blockchain technology.

People still require credit in order to run a business and survive on their own. Credit card corporations will continue to profit from transaction fees. Credits rule the globe, and capital markets will always exist within the framework of our current social order. The cost of transmitting money between groups will fall, which will benefit financial institutions. They want to focus on giving the best options in their investment or banking industries to their customers.

Bitcoin was founded as a response to the financial crisis, which led the entire economy to collapse due to fraud and other unethical behaviors. It transitions from a "trust or doesn't trust" worldview to a trustless system. Most people are unaware of this tiny distinction. A trustless system is one in which you trust and distrust everyone in the network equally. More importantly, the blockchain provides a framework for transactions to take place without the need for trust.

Blockchain ID systems will allow you to pick what information you expose to whom and at what level in the future. The more anonymous data it possesses, the more secure it is. By not sharing information with those who do not need it or have permission to see it, blockchain systems will assist to reduce identity and data theft.

Another benefit of blockchain technology is that it will move fraud from where it occurred in the past to where it is presently occurring in real time. Audits are fractional post-mortems of what has occurred in our existing system. A team of outside auditors arrives, pulls a few random files, and checks to see if everything is in order. Anything beyond this is prohibitively expensive and time-consuming. Record systems that incorporate blockchain technology will be able to audit a file as it is created, indicating incomplete or anomalous files as they are created. Managers will now have the tools they need to rectify files before they become a problem.

Another characteristic of blockchain systems will be the ability to transparently share data with external parties. In the future, sharing data will be as simple as emailing a zip file, but the recipient will have access to the original copy rather than a copy if the file is delivered by email. When someone transfers a file, he has one version on his computer, and the receiver has one as well. With blockchain technology, the two persons will only have one version to share.

Blockchains serve as a third party that verifies the age and creation of files. They can identify any individual who interacts with a file across systems, both within and externally. They can display what is missing from a file, not just the data that is already present in it. Blockchain files can also be transmitted with redactions that do not jeopardize document authenticity. This implies that you'll be able to see a file's age, complete history, and what it looked like over time as it evolved. More intriguingly, you'll be able to detect if a file is missing anything. This is known as proving the negative. Most file systems can only tell you what's inside them at this point. However, you will be able to discern what a file lacks.

Auditing will be less costly and more thorough. Audit rules could be updated in a more centralized manner. When regulatory nodes in a blockchain network have a shared and transparent picture of asset transactions, reporting of these transactions can be done through the regulator's location rather than requiring 100 or more other institutions to follow the same rule set.

Blockchain-based solutions that are fully integrated throughout a business will be able to track every dollar spent. The final mile of how money is spent is the most difficult for organizations and governments to account for. Because it is so difficult to account for, people looking to steal money have the perfect opportunity.

The last mile could be a company's best opportunity to save money and discover unethical employees. Nonprofits who have tight accounting requirements for how they spend their money could gain the most from this type of approach. They might achieve their auditing and donor accountability obligations without affecting their larger goals for good.

One technology under consideration would integrate directly into the workflow of assistance workers. This system was originally intended to maintain medical information, but it can also track all supplies used with each medical patient. Given how much fraud and theft occurs in the NGO field, the benefits of this approach would be enormous.

Future Banking Trends

Data sovereignty and digital privacy will be major problems in the future.

Because the entire economy will be using a cryptocurrency, there will always be an auditable trail inside the blockchain that secures it, making fraud prevention easier. This may be appealing to police enforcement, but it is a nightmare for consumer privacy.

From the standpoint of the customer, everything you buy with a credit or debit card already has an audit record. Audit trails are advantageous to institutions because they promote transparency of paperwork and the life cycles of these assets' travels between different areas. It lends legitimacy to asset trading and helps them to incorporate compliance into their day-to-day operations.

The European Union's "right to be forgotten" provisions, which provide citizens the right not to have their data perpetually spread on the Internet, pose a severe problem for blockchains because blockchains can never forget.

Governments and corporations would have permanent historical recordings of every transaction, which if made public may be disastrous to national security. In the case of a firm, it may provide competitors with inside information on how their competitors are investing.

The most difficult aspect of adopting a permissionless blockchain like Ethereum or Bitcoin is ensuring that you haven't transmitted money to an OFAC jurisdiction to assist terrorism. The answer is no, because they are semi-anonymous and anyone may open a wallet. It is easy to develop algorithms to track transaction movement – the US government has been doing so for years — but in a permissionless society, anyone can move value. The Office of Foreign Asset Control maintains sanctions against certain organization s or individuals in high-risk countries.

When using permissionless platforms anonymously, the government is unable to follow the history of transactions.

The requirement for KYC and AML strengthens the case for permissioned blockchain in the shared ledger environment. R3 developed Corda, a private and permissioned blockchain-like technology, to directly address several of these difficulties. They specifically do not broadcast the data from their participants globally. This protects the data on the Corda blockchain and was the key nonfunctional requirement required by the more than 75 institutions who collaborated with R3 to implement blockchain technology. They must safeguard their privacy while yet meeting stringent regulatory requirements.

Blockchain technology will usher in a slew of new forms of securities and investment products. Because collateral will be far more visible and fungible across institutions when it is accounted for within a blockchain back system, new markets will emerge with more efficient ways of measuring risk. According to Hernando de Soto, a well-known Peruvian economist, granting titles for the world's poor for their land, residences, and unregistered enterprises would unleash $9.3 trillion in assets. This is what the term "dead capital" refers to.

It is conceivable that countries that can release their dead capital, or unfinanceable real estate, will be able to bundle and sell their stakes in these assets on a worldwide scale. Transparent mortgage-backed securities for new real estate developments in Colombia or Peru, for example.

Countries will be able to free up their dead capital in the future. Owners of properties, undeveloped land, and unfinanceable properties will now be able to sell their stakes in these assets on a global scale.

These assets will be popular because asset managers will be able to actively parse underperforming assets thanks to the transparency and capability of one being substituted for another via blockchain-based technology. The use of blockchains to handle these assets will provide managers with the ability to constantly possess top-performing securities, removing bad apples, reclassifying them, and selling them as new securities.

Micro-investments will be an appealing outlet for non-institutional customers, enabled worldwide and locally by blockchain trading platforms. Using blockchain technology will also provide people with the ability to invest in firms and specialised activities without having to meet minimums or go via intermediaries that take a share of the money.

Decentralized autonomous organization s (DAOs) are now in operation, facilitating DAO investment pools for a select group of risk-averse and technically skilled investors. It may be some time before an institutional investor uses one or a portfolio manager advises her customers to invest in a DAO-based vehicle.

DAOs eliminate much of the paperwork and complexity associated with investment by establishing a blockchain-based voting system and awarding shares to individuals who invest in their product. The "code as law" approach renders any blockchain merciless. The dangers are numerous, especially when there is badly written code that executes in unexpected ways. Hacks to this system can have serious effects. The original system's transparency, as well as the weak programming, provide hackers with a wider attack vector and allow them to attack several times as they gather more and more information each time.

Our world is global, and businesses have no borders. Instant and practically free payroll is appealing and would save employers a lot of trouble. However, there are certain disadvantages. The greatest risk will be the loss of funds as a result of hacking. It would be hard to recover your assets if you were compensated in cryptocurrencies and were hacked. There is no alternative dispute resolution center. There is no way to contact customer service about the loss of these monies. Digital currency thieves have worldwide access while remaining largely anonymous. The hacker could be located anywhere.

The consumer is accountable for his own security under the existing blockchain system. Customers currently bear the primary burden of protecting and insuring themselves against loss. Larger corporations and governments have provided safety and insurance for as long as anybody can remember.

Ordinary people haven't had to safeguard themselves in this way since mediaeval times, when they stopped holding their own gold (more or less). These difficulties have not deterred businesses from embracing cryptocurrencies to manage payroll. Bitwage and BitPay are both competing in the market for Bitcoin payroll processing. Bitwage enables employees and independent contractors to get a portion of their income in bitcoin even if their employers do not provide the option. Payroll service providers Zuman and Incoin, on the other hand, are connected into BitPay's payment and payroll APIs. Again, early adoption is taking place in places where there were previously no or insufficient answers.

Blockchains will allow for speedier and potentially more inclusive trading. In recent years, global trade finance has been constrained. Some banks, such as Barclays, have even withdrawn from expanding African markets. They leave a void for trade financing. Companies continue to require capital in order to ship their goods.

DAOs and micro investments may be able to address that requirement while also providing investors with more attractive returns than are now accessible on the market. Transparency of all commodities sold, safe identity, and seamless worldwide tracking all linked to a blockchain would make this possibility available to small investors.

Interoperability of currencies, which businesses like Ripple facilitate, will also allow for more trade since they provide more flexible means of computing foreign exchange rates than transfer channels. The inclusion of more popular digital currencies in foreign currency exchanges will increase the flexibility and integration of untapped markets.

Guaranteed payments enabled by blockchain-backed transactions will boost trade in areas where confidence is low. Within these types of institutions, poorer countries can compete on the same playing field as wealthier nations. Global economies will transform as a result of this over the next ten years. Commodity and labor costs are likely to rise.

Global corporations compensate their staff depending on competitive pricing as well as historical remuneration. It will take time for blockchains to enable equality across economic differences.

Developers and other knowledge workers would be the exception, as it would be easier for them to support themselves through anonymous employment.

Financial inclusion and equal global commerce are critical issues for governments to address. Small and underdeveloped countries are more likely to adopt digital currencies on a national scale. Most major countries have dispersed power structures that make it difficult to make rapid changes to critical systems such as money.

Small countries' central power arrangements will allow them to bypass outdated infrastructure and bureaucracy. Most African and South American countries, for example, lack landlines and addresses, but they all have smartphones and the ability to build cryptocurrency wallets. The missing ingredient is overall trade liquidity and the ability to use a cryptocurrency to pay for basic requirements such as utilities, rent, and food.

Decentralized applications: Welcome to the future

The self-governing and decentralised application is Ethereum's most revolutionary and contentious expression (DAPP). DAPPs are capable of managing digital assets and DAOs.

DAPPs were intended to replace centralised asset and organization management. Because many individuals believe that absolute power corrupts absolute power, this system has a lot of appeal. This type of arrangement has tremendous ramifications for those who are afraid of losing control. DAOs are a form of Ethereum application that represents a virtual entity on the Ethereum blockchain. When you build a DAO, you can ask people to participate in the organization's governance. The participants can remain anonymous and never meet, which could raise Know Your Customer (KYC) and anti-money laundering (AML) compliance difficulties. Know Your Customer (KYC) rules (the process a corporation must go through to authenticate the identity of its clients) compliance issues.

DAOs were developed to raise capital for investment, but they might also be used for civic or charitable causes. Ethereum provides a basic governance system. It is up to the organizers to decide what is governed. Ethereum has developed templates to assist you in the development of DAOs. Unlike most typical investment vehicles, where a central entity makes investment decisions, the members of a DAO own 100% of the assets. They cast ballots on new investments and other matters. This framework has the potential to displace traditional financial managers.

DAOs are constructed with code that cannot be modified in the middle of the process. The appeal is that hostile hackers cannot manipulate the funds in the traditional sense.

Hackers can still find new ways to run the malware and withdraw payments. Because of the immutability of a DAO's code, it is nearly impossible to patch any issues once the DAO is live in Ethereum. The name of the first Ethereum DAO ever formed is, predictably, "The DAO."

It exemplifies some of the risks associated with decentralised and independent entities. It is the world's largest crowdfunded project, with over 11,000 people raising nearly $162 million in 26 days.

What was considered to be The DAO's greatest strength turned out to be its greatest flaw. The DAO's immutable code established how the company would be controlled and how funds would be dispersed. This gave the members confidence in their investment. Despite the fact that the code had been thoroughly examined, not all of the bugs had been resolved.

The DAO breach posed the first big danger to Ethereum. A previously unknown code path in The DAO's contract enabled any knowledgeable user to extract funds. An unnamed user was able to withdraw almost $50 million before being apprehended.

The Ethereum community argued vehemently on whether or not it should recapture the ether. Technically, the DAO hacker had done nothing wrong or hacked the system. Fundamentalists in the Ethereum community believed that code was law and that no action should be taken to retrieve the assets. Ethereum's greatest strength was also its greatest weakness. Because of decentralisation, immutability, and autonomy, no central authority could rapidly decide what to do. There was also no one to punish for system abuse. It had no consumer protection protections at all. It was, as the software's name promised, a new frontier.

After several weeks of deliberation, the Ethereum community chose to deactivate The DAO and launch a new Ethereum. This is known as hard forking. When the Ethereum community hard-forked the network, it reversed the hacker's transaction. It also gave birth to two Ethereums: Ethereum and Ethereum Classic. This choice did not go down well with everyone. Ethereum Classic is still in use by the community. The Ethereum Classic tokens are still traded, although their market value has dropped significantly. The new Ethereum coin has yet to regain its previous peak from before the theft. The decision to fork shook the blockchain community. It was the first time a majority blockchain project hard-forked in order to make one investor whole. Many of the ideas that make blockchain technology so appealing in the first place were called into question.

Conclusion

This toolkit is intended to serve as a starting point for policymakers wanting to understand the dangers and possibilities provided by DeFi businesses and services, as well as to develop the optimal policy responses.

The specific forms of DeFi, as well as the regulatory problems they raise, will evolve over time, as will activity levels and other aspects of the wider blockchain and digital asset universe.

Different measures will be taken by policymakers and regulators depending on the specific environment of their respective jurisdictions. Larger adjustments in financial regulatory duties, or the development of cross-national standards, may affect the framework in which DeFi concerns are considered. There were no decentralised digital currency assets prior to 2009, and no general-purpose smart contract platforms prior to 2015, therefore any recommendations regarding how to approach an offshoot like DeFi must take into account potential and unanticipated developments in a quickly expanding area.

What is evident is that DeFi is a separate and potentially significant development, both within the context of blockchain and of financial services in general. As this research has demonstrated, DeFi brings a plethora of opportunities as well as numerous problems. Even when there are no obvious answers, policymakers are best served by thinking about the relevant questions to ask, understanding the areas of interaction and tension with their regulatory regimes, and calculating the costs and advantages of various courses of action.

Decentralized finance outperforms traditional finance in the areas of decentralisation, access, efficiency, interoperability, and transparency. Decentralization allows the community to collectively own financial goods without top-down control, which could be dangerous to the typical consumer. Access to these new products for all persons is crucial to keeping wealth disparities from expanding.

Traditional finance has layers of fat and inefficiency that ultimately deprive the common consumer of value. DeFi's contractual efficiency returns all of this value.

Because of its shared architecture and interfaces, DeFi enables extreme interoperability that would be impossible to achieve in traditional finance. Finally, the open nature of DeFi increases confidence and security in places where there has traditionally been opacity.

DeFi can also actively provide value to users to stimulate its expansion, as Compound (through COMP) and Uniswap have done (via UNI). Yield farming is the practice of obtaining rewards by putting funds into platforms that provide incentives for liquidity provisioning. Token distributions and yield farming have drew significant sums of capital to DeFi in remarkably short periods of time. Platforms may design their token economics to promote innovation while also fostering a long-term sustainable protocol and community that continues to generate value.

Each DeFi use case exemplifies some of these benefits more than others while also posing significant limitations and risks. For example, a DeFi network that primarily relies on a centralised oracle will never be as decentralised as a platform that requires no external input to run, such as Uniswap. Furthermore, a platform with some off-chain infrastructure in its exchange, such as dYdX, cannot have the same levels of openness and interoperability.

Certain hazards afflict all of DeFi, and overcoming them is critical to DeFi's general adoption. Scaling risk and smart contract risk are two specific dangers. If the underlying technology cannot scale to service the entire population, the benefits of DeFi will be limited to only the wealthiest parties. Inevitably, scaling solutions will come at the expense of some of the advantages of a "pure" DeFi approach, such as diminished interoperability on a "sharded" blockchain. The benefits and scalability will improve over time, as they have with the internet and other breakthrough technologies. Smart contract risk will never be removed, but experience will guide best practices and industry trends in the future.

As a warning to dApps that blindly merge and build on top of one other without due diligence, the weakest link in the chain will bring the entire house down. The severity of smart contract risk increases in direct proportion to the natural proclivity to innovate and integrate with new technology.

As a result, high-profile flaws will continue to imperil user funds, as they have in the past. If DeFi cannot overcome these and other challenges, its utility will remain a shadow of its potential.

DeFi's true potential is transformational. Firms that fail to change will be lost and forgotten if DeFi fulfils its full potential. As the legislative framework becomes clearer and the risks become more known, all traditional finance institutions may and should begin to combine their services with crypto and DeFi.

Printed in Great Britain
by Amazon